THE VOICE THAT THUNDERS

Alan Garner

THE VOICE
THAT THUNDERS

ESSAYS AND LECTURES

THE HARVILL PRESS
LONDON

First published in Great Britain in 1997 by The Harvill Press

This hardback edition published in 1998 by The Harvill Press
2 Aztec Row
Berners Road
London N1 0PW

www.harvill-press.com

1 3 5 7 9 8 6 4 2

The oak spade on page 187 is reproduced from *The Jottings of some Geological,
Archaeological, Botanical, Ornithological and Zoological Rambles round Macclesfield*,
by J. D. Sainter, Macclesfield, 1878, courtesy of the British Library

A CIP catalogue record for this book
is available from the British Library

ISBN 1 86046 468 8

Designed and typeset in Joanna at
Libanus Press, Marlborough, Wiltshire

Printed and bound in Great Britain by Butler & Tanner Ltd
at Selwood Printing, Burgess Hill

For *Griselda*

"A person doesn't need to go to college to learn facts.
He can get them from books"

Albert Einstein

"Doing's a hard school, but a fool will learn at no other."

Joseph Garner, 1875–1955, whitesmith

INTRODUCTION

This book is made from various attempts to record the excitement that has attended life so far. Spread over some thirty years and now put together as one statement, they may show the progression, or otherwise, of a writer's thought, and the environment that engenders and shapes, but must never appear in, the work.

The texts are the full texts as they were written, though not always as they were presented. Lectures are constrained by time and the patience of an audience, and articles are subject to an imposed length.

I myself have edited occasionally here, but, I hope, honourably. When dealing, over time, with linked themes, it is natural if for once something has been said definitively to use it again. Therefore in this context I have avoided the inelegance that would engender. There are other kinds of repetition that may be instructive; and I have held my pen and kept them in.

So here, for me, are the building blocks of what matters. It is a map of a journey that has been made possible by the friends, influencing minds and helpers that have brought me to this point. To try to list them would be prodigal of paper beyond the reckless, and would face me with choices to defeat Solomon; for I have been most fortunate in the net of fellowship through life and around the world. Better that both fellowship and trees stand.

A.G.
Blackden
14 January 1997

THE VOICE THAT THUNDERS

1

The Edge of the Ceiling

My name is Alan Garner, and I was born, with the cord wrapped twice round my throat, in the front bedroom of 47 Crescent Road, Congleton, Cheshire, at Latitude 53° 09′40″ N, Longitude 02° 13′7″ W, at 21.30 on Wednesday, 17 October 1934. My mother was a tailor, and my father a painter and decorator.*

My mother's family were talented cranks, on every side; lateral thinking was a part of their equipment, and those that got away with it were respectable as well. Even the names are odd. There was a great-aunt Sophia Pitchfork; and a great-great-grand-uncle, J. Sparkes Hall, an inventor, of 308 & 310 Regent Street, London, Bootmaker to Her Majesty The Queen and Their Royal Highnesses The Prince and Princess of Wales. He designed the elastic-sided boot, and demonstrated his English Cottage or Test House (which became the traditional nineteenth-century worker's kitchen fire-cum-oven-cum-boiler) at the Paris Exhibition of 1867. His brother, Edward, designed and built church organs in Birkenhead.

Perhaps a more typical gene was represented by the third brother, who was Professor of Systematic Memory, or Polymnemonics, on which he delivered lectures, "copiously illustrated by Novel, Curious, Extraordinary and Interesting Experiments (Schools at halfprices)".

In the eighteenth century, the Halls cover their traces, but documentary fragments and early photographs suggest that a

* This lecture was delivered at the National Word Festival, the Australian National University, Canberra, on 21 March 1983.

3

pawnbroker Hall, of Plymouth, had fashionable tastes; and so my great-great-great-great-grandmother may have been West African.

My father's family is quite different. They have been craftsmen for centuries. They have married locally, under strict cultural tabus, and have lived in the same house without a break of tenancy. My cousin lives there now. The house stands in a small area called The Hough, on the slopes of Alderley Edge, a wooded sandstone hill above the Cheshire Plain. The Edge is a Beauty Spot in summer and at weekends, but its long history and prehistory make it unsafe at all times. It is physically and emotionally dangerous. No one born to the Edge questions that, and we show it a proper respect.

So there are three main elements in me from the start. Families on the one side gifted, unstable, and, on the other, skilled, steady. And a hill that Garners have inhabited, and worked, for as long as anybody knows.

Born in Congleton, raised in Alderley, I have lived, since 1957, seven miles from both, near the Jodrell Bank radio telescope, in a mediaeval timber-framed house on a site that has almost certainly been occupied by the living for seven thousand years, since the Mesolithic period, and by the dead as well. The mound that the house stands on is one of a group of tumuli. If I have any real occupation, it is to be here.

Therefore, I have spent the whole of my life, so far, on the Pennine shelf of East Cheshire. It is an area that encompasses most of the landscapes to be found in Britain. Within twelve miles, I can move through fen, dairy and arable farms, to sheep runs and bleak mountain tors. And, in this particular place, I find a universality that enables me to write. Everywhere is special, in some way. It was not imperative that I should be born in Cheshire; but it was imperative that I should know my place. That can be achieved only by inheriting one's childhood landscape, and by growing in it to maturity. It is a subtle matter of owning and of being owned.

The landscape of childhood is itself unremarkable, for the child.

Lack of any concept of things being other than they are found to be brings to childhood an innocence that hindsight can abuse. When we comment on the resilience of children, we should remember that what may now appear to have been brave or terrible was possibly unquestioned at the time. It was certainly unquestioned by me as an individual and by the generation of village children to which I belonged.

"God bless Mummy, God bless Daddy, make me a good boy and don't let the war end. Amen." I gabbled that prayer every night from the age of six until God let me down in 1945, when I was nearly eleven. We were not a religious family. The first three pious requests were taught by my mother, who was enlisting the Holy Trinity as a child-minder, and the last bit was my own, because I had worked out that peace would axe my favourite wireless programmes.

The knowing innocence of childhood makes something peculiar of war. Lack of experience turns it into a bright game. There is no responsibility, no foresight, no sense of deprivation. The child is free to take what he wants from the mess; and the child is a callous animal, with little built-in morality.

For us, the past was something called Pre-war. It seemed to have been an age of plenty. Adults would thumb through old mail order catalogues and talk of the good days. If the past was Pre-war, the future had no name. We were living in a geological time span called the Duration.

The nearest I came to an understanding was that I was between two periods, of which adults were aware, but I could not be: the Eldorado of Pre-war, of which I remembered only the vivid yellow and the taste and shape of a banana, and a return to an Elysium after the Duration: a "once and future peace". I felt no sense of loss.

We lived a rural life on the edge of suburbia, far enough from Manchester for us to take their evacuees, but among the anti-aircraft batteries, and where the bombers would jettison for the dash home. I lay in bed, listening. Heinkel? Dornier? It was the wah-wah of German engines as the planes dragged their weight to Manchester. Then the guns. Out of bed and into the road to pick up hot shrapnel: metal with a texture like no other: steel sand.

Next morning we would swap our shrapnel and barter for sticky incendiary bombs that were more like bicycle pumps than fireworks. For some reason, shrapnel that had been "hot-found" was worth more than "cold-found", though there was nothing by which to tell the difference now. It was a matter of unquestioned honour: the only instance that was never challenged, in my experience of childhood.

The Polish pilot would have been our greatest prize, but we lost him. His fighter was in trouble, and he crash-landed. He was dead when we arrived. We could not get the cockpit fully open before the fire reached the ammunition, and we had to leave his goggles and make do with a yellow handkerchief that had been around his neck. But the blood was real.

Our war was with the evacuees. We had them from Liverpool, Manchester, London and the Channel Islands. The worst were the Islanders. They were silent, foreign, could speak a secret language, and would not go home. Manchester, Liverpool and London fought dirty, but were scared both of woods and of open spaces. For us, a field was certain refuge from pursuit even if it were empty. The possibility of a cow lurking in the cropped grass was something that no townie would risk.

The adult plans for what they called the Home Front (there appeared to be no Home Back; or, if there was, it did not concern them), were varied and improvised. My mother concocted the following stratagem against invasion while my father was guarding us from the Hun in Rhyl.

I kept a bag of pepper by the door, next to Mum's poker. They were for the German paratrooper. When he knocked on the door, I was going to throw the pepper into his face, Mum would hit him with the poker, and then we would run upstairs and commit suicide by hurling ourselves head first from the bedroom window. That the window was only some nine feet above the ground, with stone mullions that would have made "hurling" a problem did not make either of us question the efficacy of the scheme.

As for political understanding, I relied on the propaganda of the *Beano* and the *Dandy*: Musso the Wop (He's a Bigga-da-Flop), and Adolf and Hermie (The Nasty Nazis) in their endless search for food. "I have der pain in der breadbasket."

Peace, I thought, came when a sailor gave me a banana. But it was green. He told me that it was not ripe. I put it on the mantelpiece and watched it every day. When it was the yellow I remembered, and the smell was as I remembered, I peeled and ate it in a Proustian orgy. At that instant of biting into the fruit, I knew that the Duration was over. By colour, taste, smell and geometry, a banana, for me, bracketed the Second World War. Then everything changed.

The Belsen films were shown at our cinema. Although children were forbidden entry, we had always known the free way in. I saw the films four times. The not-dead corpse in the black skull-cap, picking over his shirt and grinning at the camera that had come too late; the bulldozer ploughing its graceful, hideous choreography into the mass grave. It was right for us to see this, to remind us that what we children were playing was being played better by adults, because they were bigger and had more toys.

Everyone will have been affected. For me, I am not afraid of the dark, and the blackout gave me a childhood of stars. But I do wish that air-raid sirens were not still used to call out the fire brigade. Also, to grow up in an improvised world, where others are trying to kill you, develops an ability to distinguish between necessity and luxury, to arrive quickly at priorities, to survive.

My children are secure in a way that we never were. They are in a saner world, though it is not sane yet. And there is a factor to consider. The Blitz, the bag of pepper, the dead pilot meant little. Belsen made sense. At the age of ten, I realised what all the fuss had been about. It was about the ovens and the people inside. Before seeing them, I knew a lot of facts, but could not give them a context. Then, within minutes, the facts came together in an image and I was violently wise. My children and their generation have not had that shock; yet they are better informed than I was, and they are better informed because they have watched television.

Rubbish, though it very often is, trite, though it nearly always is, there remains an argument for accepting the medium of television as the main cultural development of the century. It removes more barriers than it creates, and exposes liars more clearly than any previous news machine. As long as politicians and generals continue to fear the lens, and there are men and women willing to be killed serving it, future cameras may arrive in time for the not-dead corpse in the black skull-cap.

I find this hard to explain to many people, who say that the world is getting worse because what they see on the news is so terrible. I try to explain that what they see has always gone on, but they have not been able to see it as it is happening, edited, focused. If a camera had been around to record how Athens dealt with an Aegean island that objected to paying taxes, the Parthenon and our model of Western thought would have been put into a different perspective indeed. This century has moved the portrayal of war from static engravings, with no corpses, in the *Illustrated London News*, of events long gone and in another country, to a young girl running naked in napalm into your house, in high-quality colour, and now.

Television removes barriers. My attitudes in childhood were partly the innate callousness of an infant, and the war ended when I was on the threshold of adolescence, ready to become more aware of other people. I maintain that children now are more aware, more humane, because they have learned more through television than we did by living in an isolation that happened to be punctuated by random, and occasional, violence close at hand.

I would say that television presents facts and offers interpretation in a way that involves every area of our lives. Of course it can be, and is, abused; but I had to grub among old cigarette cards to extend my knowledge. Set that against what is available now. Rubbish there was, is and ever shall be. What has to be educated is choice. That is the difference. My children are richer in mind and spirit than I was, and from that richness grows compassion.

Let me stress that I see no miracle, no sudden generation of angels. But, where I tried to snatch the pilot's goggles, the next children may not let him put them on.

So, while Leningrad starved for nine hundred days and Belsen conducted its roaring trade, my childhood was happy, along with the other village children; and, in addition, unaware that all children did not commonly live as I lived, I spent ten years in two worlds.

The daily landscape for me was a bedroom ceiling in a brick cottage, with a porch. It became the house of Elidor, and the porch the entrance to the Mound of Vandwy, "night's dungeon", because it was out of that porch my father stepped one January in the pre-dawn blackness and disappeared to join the army while my mother and I cried, certain we should not see him again.

The bedroom was whitewashed, irregular plaster, steeply pitched, with rafters and purlins and ridge exposed. And I lay on my back beneath it through three long illnesses: diphtheria, meningitis and pneumonia.

I had no brothers or sisters. The Second World War came and went. The family survived. There were no tragedies. But the isolation caused by physical weakness and paralysis must have been increased by the more general isolation of a house threatened, bombed, blacked out. When I was bedfast, the rhythms of day and night were not imposed on me. Rather than sleep, I catnapped, or was in coma. Reality was the room.

The view from my window was, for five years, glued over with cheesecloth against bomb blast; but, even unrestricted, it was no more than a length of road where little happened, and which was closed by the spire and weathercock of a Victorian church, on which my great-great-grandfather had worked, and later became a running stitch through *The Stone Book Quartet*. Sideways rolling of my head made the spire wobble, the houses insecure, and people on the road change shape. I knew that the uneven window pane was the cause, but it still gave the room the greater reality. The ceiling did not wobble when I rolled my head.

There was a forest in the ceiling, with hills and clouds, and a road to the horizon. The way into the ceiling for me was harder at some times than at others. To enter the ceiling, I had to stare at the road and remove detail from the sides of vision by unfocusing my eyes. I had to block sound. I had to switch myself off.

"Switching off" is not a good description, because there was a profound engagement in the activity of making the bed-bound "me" let go of me. The changes in sound and vision were felt by the "me" on the bed. I had to remove myself from that. I would concentrate on the concentration of the "me" concentrating. I thought of the thought of myself thinking. I observed the observer observing; until the observer was not the observed.

Whatever actually took place, the sensation was that of sliding out of phase with the boy in the bed. And the automatic result was to find that I had crossed the neutralised zone from the bed into the ceiling. I did not sleep. There was no relaxing of consciousness. It was the opposite. I had to think harder, relatively, than at any previous time of my life. The thoughts may have been unusual, but the thinking was not.

I could tell the difference between waking and sleeping because of something else that developed. It was the ability to programme myself for dreaming before I slept, rather like choosing from a menu. Generally, the dreams would come in their programmed order, though nightmares were frequent and unsought.

If I found myself in a nightmare, I would first check that I was dreaming, then watch for the approach of the nightmare's particular horror, and jump headfirst into it to wake myself up. I always knew when I was dreaming, because I could control the dream. The ceiling, however, I could not predict. Once I was on the road in the ceiling, there was no effort needed to keep me there. I entered, and did not look back. I did not see the boy on the bed. I felt that I was awake.

The world of the ceiling was three-dimensional, objects were solid, visual perspectives true. I never ate or drank in the ceiling (as I later found was the rule for the Other World). There was no wind, no climate, no heat, no cold, no time. The light came from no source and was shadowless, as neon; but before I knew neon. And everywhere, everybody, everything was white. It was the genesis of the dead land of Elidor.

Another peculiarity was that I could see in the dark. If I lay in bed, in the black room, the ceiling became fluorescent, or a negative film. And, when I went into the ceiling, the ceiling-world was lit by the same reversed light, and so were the people and so was I. Otherwise, the ceiling was, for me, "natural". I met people I knew, including my parents, and some who were only of the ceiling. None of the "ceiling people" has turned up in later life, yet, and they had no names. The people I knew in both states of waking had no knowledge of the ceiling when I asked them. I soon stopped asking.

Of course, this is interpretation now. I should not have been able to describe the ceiling in these words at the age when I lived there. I "lived" in the ceiling. But there was a difference between the ceiling and the bed that made the bed, with all its pain and debility, the permanent choice.

Although the way to the ceiling was along the same road in

the ceiling, the land beyond the road, from visit to visit, was inconsistent; and this inconsistency made the ceiling not more interesting but less. Each venture was separate rather than a learning, and such variety leads nowhere; it builds nothing; it has nothing to teach. And I wanted to learn. That was the difference. I would enter the ceiling by an act of will, but I left it through tedium. Sooner or later, I would stop whatever I was doing in the ceiling, turn around, and always be facing the same road-forest-cloud-hill picture that I saw from my bed. Then I would pull back as a camera does to the bed and lie looking at the lime-washed plaster.

There was one terror in the ceiling: one motionless dread.

Sometimes I would look up, and see no road, no forest, clouds or hills, but a plump little old woman with a circular face, hair parted down the middle and drawn to a tight bun, lips pursed, and small, pebbled eyes. She sat wrapped in a shawl in a cane wheelchair and watched me. She was a waning moon: her head turned to the side, as if she had broken her neck. When I saw her, I knew that I could die. She must not enter the room, and I must not enter the ceiling. If I let her eyes blink, I should die. There was no night, day, dawn, dusk. The little old woman and I were locked.

The little old woman came only when my life really was threatened. She was a part of the plaster in the ceiling, not of my room but of my parents' room, and I was taken there when I was too ill to be left alone. She was my death, and I knew it.

One hundred and fifty yards from bed, and behind the house, was my other world. Later knowledge told me that it was an eroded fault-scarp, 600 feet high, of the Keuper and Bunter Triassic sandstones. To me, it was the Edge, that cliff covered with trees, mined for copper and quarried for stone through centuries and then abandoned. When I was not confined to the house, I would spend my days and my nights on the Edge.

Woodland on a crag of coloured stone was just the beginning of that world for me. In the best sense, as a family, we have always known our place. We handled it as miners and stone-cutters. We culled its timber for houses and fuel, and grew food on its soil. At a deeper level, we accepted that there was a Hero King asleep in the ground, behind a rock named the Iron Gates. Our water supply derived from the Holy Well, which granted wishes to tourists at weekends, and an income for the child of our family who, on a Monday morning, cleaned out the small change.

Yet for no money would that child have climbed the yew that stood beside the well. "If I ever so much as see you touch that," my grandfather said, "I'll have the hide off you." And there was a memory that could hardly be restored to words: of how the well was not for wishing, but for the curing of barren women; and the offerings were of bent pins, not of pence. And Grandad spoke of rags tied to trees there. That had been a long time ago, he said.

So it is for a child born to the Edge. We knew our place, and knowledge passed beyond the material, such as where a band of white clay was under the fallen leaves which could be used as soap to clean up with before going home. It passed to the spiritual, too. I was brought up to respect both. They were there. Even the ghosts were those of relatives.

Yet my relationship with that hill was different from that of the rest of my family. As a result of gained knowledge, for me the Edge both stopped, and melted, time.

I knew enough geology to become amazed. I could trace the tidal vortex in the strata: the print of water swirling for a second under the pull of wind and moon and held for two hundred million years. I felt the white pebbles in the rock, and wondered from what mountains they had come, by what river, to what sea.

And, in the fleeting, I found the vision. In knowing the moment of the vortex, and of the pebble, which, if I could have watched for long enough, was not rock but liquid, I lost all sense of "me" upon the hill. As with the ceiling, a barrier was down. But, perhaps because I was not weakened, fevered, paralysed, the result was different. I felt not that I entered a world, but that a world entered me. There were no exploits such as the ceiling gave; no journeys; no people. Of the two landscapes, the ceiling was the more mundane. But the ceiling had showed me that time was not simply a clock; and so I was open to the hill and to the metaphors of time that the hill gave. And the years of bed had developed another freedom.

For most children, I know now, time drags. That is because inertia is uncommon, and days are filled with events. But where a child has only inertia, time must not rule. And I played with time as if it were chewing-gum, making a minute last an hour, and a day compress to a minute. I had to. If I had not kept time pliant, it would have set me as the pebble in the rock.

So I brought to the coloured cliff and my strength the craft of the white ceiling and my weakness. I switched myself off. And the universe opened. I was shown a totality of space and time, a kaleidoscope of images expanding so quickly that they fragmented. There were too many, too fast for individual detail or recall. They dropped below the subliminal boundary, but I felt the rip-tide of their surge, and the rip-tide has remained.

Yet despite the hurly-burly beyond words, when I partook of the hill and the hill partook of me, there was a calm, which childhood could not give. For if the child had been left with only a vision, if the "me" had not been replaced by a truer sense of self, I do not know what would have happened. I do not know that I could have grown. With only a blind vision, I do not know that I could have survived.

I said at the beginning that, as children, we accept "normality" to be whatever is around us; and I have tried to describe three experiences to demonstrate what I mean. Man, though, at every age is also an animal with instincts that need no teaching; and the strongest instinct is for life. Yet in childhood, at three separate times I died.

It was not medical death in the way that it can now be defined. It was the opinion of doctors, humane men, around the bed of an organism under the rough ceiling of a cottage below Alderley Edge. The child was technically alive, but all his systems were collapsing, and there was nothing more to be done for him. In one instance, meningitis, I heard my mother being helped to accept the imminent death by being told that for me to recover would be a cruelty, because the damage to brain and spine would be massive, and I should be a bedridden thing for the rest of my life: not a person, not a son.

What those humane men did not take into account was that I was not yet dead. I could not signal, I was unable to communicate with the outside world, but I was not yet dead. I could hear. And I heard. I heard myself dismissed, written off. It was, to the animal in me, an attempt to kill my life.

I screamed, using no words, making no sound. The body was nearly dead. But fury then was greater than death, and, though nothing showed on the surface of the creature under the sheet, inside was war. I raged against the cosmos. Inside me was a zoo gone mad. Outside was calm, immobile, good-as-dead. And that is why I lived. I was too angry to die.

Mine was a glorious childhood. I would not wish it on anyone, nor on me again. But it happened. And my good fortune was that I was able, as a child, to know my death, to face the ultimate, before experience scrambled my brains.

I am not arguing for life-at-all-costs. I hope I am not so arrogant that I would even begin to tell other people in other circumstances what to do. Indeed, I am at a disadvantage. I have known my death and known its ways, but I have never felt so desperate that I have wanted to die. I have felt so desperate that I have wanted to live. I have pursued life through the Edge and the ceiling and am simply relating a number of connected events that, though personal to me, may by their simplicity be of interest to others.

I speak as a survivor, and have described some techniques of survival, the pursuit of life, through the Edge and the ceiling, through inner and outer space and time, which I used as a child at an historic period when strangers were trying to kill me. The instincts were those of an animal, but they went on to teach me something more. They taught me that we transcend technique and that all experience can be made positive and turned to good. But we can never afford to stop.

If I had stopped, having survived, the technique of the Edge and the ceiling might have dwindled into a sloppy mysticism; but instead I endured the rigours of an education that matched vision with thought, each to feed the other, so that dream and logic both had their place, both made sense, and legend and history could both be true.

In such a way, one mere survival was transcended, and is to this day. Each connection seen brings greater awe. My privileged childhood forced me to choose whether to live or to die; and I saw that inner and outer worlds did not collide. I saw a unity at work outside myself.

I have often been asked by people who know this history whether that childhood made me a writer. If I had not had the encounter with my death and the Damascan road provided by the Edge, would I have been granted the vision needed in order to write? If I had not been born with the stamina of will and the bloody-mindedness required of all writing, should I have meekly accepted the doctors' diagnosis? All I can say is that many writers have been only children, and have suffered long and life-threatening illness in isolation from human company.

My wife has voiced a theory that may well be of literary import in the context of my experience at that given time. She is a teacher and critic, and we argue endlessly, within a framework of general agreement. So I may put forward these thoughts without much fear of misrepresentation; and you may be sure that she will have checked them before they are spoken, since she says that, if a fiction can improve on the fact, I shall always chose the fiction. She claims to find, in recent children's literature, little that qualifies as literature. She asked herself why this should be, after a Golden Age that ran from the late Fifties to the late Sixties. And she found that generally the writers of this Golden Age were children during the Second World War: a war waged against civilians.

The atmosphere that these children and young people grew up in was one of a whole community and a whole nation united against pure evil, made manifest in the person of Hitler. Parents were seen to be afraid. Death was a constant possibility. There was no expectation of security. The talk was of an idyllic time in the past, and the propaganda promised a better future.

Therefore, daily life was lived on a mythic plane: of absolute Good against absolute Evil; of the need to endure, to survive whatever had to be overcome, to be tempered in whatever furnace was required. These are spiritual, moral and philosophical issues, and, therefore, bound to have had an effect on the psyche of childhood at that time.

Those children who were born writers, and who would be adolescent when the full horrors became known, would not be able to avoid concerning themselves with the issues; and so their books, however clad, were written on profound themes, and were literature. The generation that has followed is not so fuelled, and its writing is, by comparison, effete and trivial.

Susan Cooper, an exact contemporary of mine at Oxford, has said: "I know that the shape of my imagination, and all its unconscious preoccupations, were moulded by having been a child in the war."

At a deeper level, and more enigmatically, Kurt Hahn said in 1947: "Education has no nobler task than to provide the moral equivalent of war."

So far my wife. I can testify to the weight of at least one part of her observations. She is right in saying that we were living on a mythic plane. I remember the frequency with which the Sleeping Hero under the hill behind the village was referred to by adults. They said of him, half (yet only half) in jest, that, since he was waiting to ride out when England should be "in direst peril", and, "in a battle thrice lost, thrice won, drive the enemy into the sea", it was about time for him to be doing. It showed me at an early age the enduring power of myth. In 1940 it was something the village turned to seriously.

I would add on my own account that, when I see the materialistic brats who have never had to ask twice to be appeased muling and puling now as adults, I agree with Othello that "the tyrant custom . . . hath made the flinty and steel couch of war my thrice-driven bed of down". Richard Crawshaw's, ". . . all wonders in one sight. Eternity shut in a span." That was what I felt on that bed.

Educationalist and critic may dispute the matter; psychologist and philosopher, biologist and theologian, too. For me, there is no conflict. I am a writer. It is enough that as a child I saw, and came to know, my place.

2

Aback of Beyond

Death's visitations in the lower stages of society do not generally call forth
much, if any, public notice, even in a country district. In the case of Garner,
a humble stone-cutter, we find something of an exception to the general rule.
He was born, brought up, and he lived until his death at the old cottage at
the foot of the Edge, near the Hough Chapel. While following with zeal his
humble trade, he associated himself with finer things in leisure hours. He was
a lover of music. The old Hough Band owes its existence in no small measure
to Garner. In numerous other ways were he and his music noticed and
known. He was not only a ringer and a singer, but he and his ophicleide will
be missed at sacred gatherings about the district.*

We are addressing ourselves to "The Development of the Spiritual",
and one cause of my having a claim to your time and attention
today has its beginning not in 1996, but in 1893, which is the
date of the obituary notice of my great-great-grandfather, Robert,
a part of which I have just read to you.

My father kept the fragile cutting in his wallet, and would take
it out and declaim it with pride: pride that the family name had
got into the local newspaper. For me, aged about nine when I first
heard it, there was only an unarticulated sense of imprisonment, of
condescension. And no one could tell me what an ophicleide was.

* This lecture was first delivered at the the Annual Conference of The Society
of Headmasters and Headmistresses of Independent Schools, at Breadsall Priory,
6 March 1996 (an extended version of the address given to the Headmasters'
Conference, Cambridge, 1991).

Now I'm going to tell you a story.

If you don't like, don't listen, as Russian fairy tales begin: but once upon a time, not near, not far, not high, not low, beyond thrice nine lands, beyond the tenth kingdom, a young man sat on a tree stump. His name was not Jack, but Alan, because the young man was me.

I sat in turmoil. The trouble was that within me were two people. One was the son of a family of rural craftsmen. They had shaped the place in which I had grown; everywhere I turned, their hands showed me their skills; yet my hands had no cunning; with them I could make nothing, and my family despaired of me.

The other me was different. He was not the first of that family to be intelligent, but he was the first to be taught. I had gone to Manchester Grammar School and to Oxford University, to be made adept in Latin, Greek, Ancient History and Philosophy: to be versed in Western Classical Humanism. And in this world I had flourished, and had long had one ambition: the Chair of Greek at Oxford. But something had gone wrong.

My military service had made me lose confidence in my motives. I could no longer be certain whether ambition was being driven by a love for Greek or by a disguised wish for power, or both. If it were Greek I wanted, then I could as well settle on Orkney, where, at least, the tide delivers free coal twice daily from the bunkers of the scuttled German fleet. Being a Professor entailed, along with power, a lack of freedom, which was more than important to me.

I had read my *Republic*: "The biggest loss, if a man himself will not rule, is to be ruled by someone worse." And John Stuart Mill: "The proper person to be entrusted with power is the person most unwilling to accept it." But I had left the army swearing never again to oblige anybody to do anything against their will. The army's "Man Management" course had confirmed me in this, where we were told that it was better to give an order, and to get it wrong, than to vacillate, and get it right. I had put this theory into practice one morning when I had deployed a troop of artillery along Guildford's busy High Street. As the traffic locked, and the police grew acerbic, and my fellow cadets sceptical, and no other members of the Royal Regiment appeared, I became more nonchalant and at the same time forceful; until one of the drivers took me aside and said: "Look, Sir, we're supposed to be on Salisbury Plain. It always is on Tuesdays."

I later worked out that, having arrived at the wrong coordinates, if I had fired the guns, and they had been accurately laid, I should have eliminated my Officers' Mess at Aldershot.

It was not only the experience of the army that made me question my motives and my future. The disturbance went much deeper. Simply, the price was too great. In order to fulfil one part of myself, I should have to kill the other; and that I could not, would not, do. To become a whole, mature and educated human being, I had to unite my divided spiritual self. I felt an anger, at once personal, social, political, philosophical and linguistic. I knew, even as I sat on the tree stump, that to express that anger directly would be negative and destructive; and I came from a family of makers, not breakers. The anger had to be a creative act.

Close by the tree stump was a stone wall. My great-great-grandfather, that Robert of the ophicleide, had built it. He had done more than that. There were tales about him, a whole culture, that must not be lost but that no one would bear witness to. He had cut a road through rock with a chisel. He had rung the bells for Saint Mary's church, and had seen to the building of the Hough Wesleyan chapel, led its music, composed it even, "while," he said, "listening to the zephyrs in the trees: always in the minor key". He had formed the Hough Temperance Band, as it was called on Sundays. During the week, they were the Hough Fizzers, and would go busking around the farms at night for money to spend at the Bull's Head. The same man played under Sir Charles Hallé in the great period of Manchester's Liberalism. Wherever the music was, there he would be.

The tales of him were endless; some struck a desperate note. He had once won an argument about the shape of Australia by drawing a map: not necessarily *the* map: a map. It was enough that he had drawn one. Given his undoubted intelligence, the implications of loss are tragic. I sat on the tree stump and looked at Robert's wall. I had to read it.

The Hough is an area at the foot of Alderley Edge, a wooded scarp in Cheshire. It has a ferocious caste system. There are four farming families, who interbreed without any apparent harm. Then there are the craft families, the Houghites, who service the community. Below the Hough stretches Lifeless Moss, bad land, fit only for the hovels of the unskilled families, the Mossaggots, and now the houses of Manchester's stockbrokers. The Houghites have a terrible fear of being polluted by the Mossaggots. I was not allowed to play with their children. Yet Robert Garner's favourite daughter Mary fell in love with Joseph Clewes, Mossaggot, and had a son by him. Robert forbade the marriage, expelled his daughter, and he and his wife brought up the boy, my grandfather Joseph, themselves. He was thus a "grannyreardun"; and the shame of his birth affected the rest of her life. In the words of my grandfather, "She never put her bonnet on again." That is, she never left the confines of the garden. She felt the taint of Mossaggotry till death.

There is a particular pride amongst the Houghites. Each generation feels obliged to better, or do other than, the one before. It is called "getting aback of". And what could Joseph get aback of with such a grandfather?

Joseph was very intelligent. He was so intelligent that the Vicar allowed him to leave school at the age of nine, three years early, because he had learnt all that was required of his future station: he could read, and he could write and he could count. And he got aback of old Robert. He became a smith, or rather two smiths, by being apprenticed twice: as a blacksmith, who works in hard metals, and a whitesmith, who works in soft. "The smith's aback of beyond!" he used to say. "Who else can make the tools?"

Joseph's intelligence went partly into his work. He developed skills that he would not teach his apprentices, secrets of applied metallurgy that died with him. He was also obsessed by number. It was exactly a mile from the house to the smithy, and he told me, when he retired, that he had ridden his bicycle the equivalent of two and a half times around the circumference of the earth at the Equator, between home and work. In the First World War, he had used fifteen tons of iron in making thirty-three thousand six hundred shoes for eight thousand four hundred horses. And he had a hobby.

In the days when the London Omnibus Service published a timetable, he would memorise it, and subscribed to each revision, so that he was always up to date. He went to London only once, and my grandmother said it was like having her own private limousine. She saw all of London, and never had to wait for a bus, because Joe carried everything in his head. It was another chilling waste, more complex, but no better, than drawing an alleged map.

My grandfather and I got on well. A craftsman never praises, but there was a rough warmth towards me, and I would spend hours in the glow of his smithy, sharing a keg of beer, listening to his exploits and the scandals of the village.

We met at a point that neither of us could have seen. During the Second World War, children had to have their names on all their clothing, and my grandfather stamped mine on the wooden soles of my clogs with the punches he used for labelling farmers' milk churns. "I reckon I've come near on writing a book with these," he said.

I was fortunate enough to be ill for most of my primary school years, sometimes spectacularly so. I was in hospital with meningitis when I learnt to read. It was the back page of the Knockout comic, alas now long defunct, but quite as good as the *Beano* and the *Dandy*. The back page was Stonehenge Kit, the Ancient Brit, who every week had to overcome the wiles of Willie the Wicked Wizard. And, one awesome day, I realised that the little bugs in the balloons related to, and commented on and expanded the pictures in the frames. From that moment everything was swallowed whole. Understanding didn't matter. I binged on words.

When I was recovering at home, my teacher Miss Bratt arrived with a pack of reading cards for me, because she was troubled that I should be falling so far behind. I remember my mother conducting a filibuster at the door, so that Miss Bratt would not see me lying on the sofa, reading *Dombey and Son*. And, at school, inside my *Milly-Molly-Mandy* class reader, would be hidden *Tarzan of the Apes* or *The Saint Goes West*.

What I saw of school I hated. And what they saw of me was liked no better. I did not further my cause. I was either not present in school, or, though underperforming through frustration, top of the class when I was there. I was helped a great deal by the BBC Schools' Service, for which, in order not to miss an episode, I learnt how to fake symptoms of complex diseases, and by my maternal grandmother's eight volumes of Arthur Mee's 1908 *Children's Encyclopaedia*, with which I was as thorough as my grandfather had been with the London Omnibus timetable. When I did appear at school I would endear myself to my comrades by drawing detailed sections through a volcano, to their great interest; as a result of which I discovered, at an early age, that I was a natural athlete, because they never could catch me between the school gates and home.

At a later stage when I went before the War Office Selection Board for them to decide whether or not I was "officer material" Arthur Mee was invaluable to me. Among the tests of our abilities was one that was critical, where we were individually responsible for the success or failure of our team in the solution of a problem.

I was not sanguine about the moment when I should be given my task. It turned out to be Arthur Mee's "How-Does-Mary-Get-the-Eggs?" (Vol.1, p.116.)* I was canny enough to go through the motions of thought before solving the problem, and that, I later discovered, was one of the two reasons why I was recommended. The other was an answer I gave in the all-important interview. When I later met the officer who had conducted it, he remembered me because in the years he had done the job, he said I was one of the only two would-be cadets who had given an honest answer to the question: "Why do you want to be an officer?" I said, "Because I can't stand wearing these hairy shirts."

A craftsman never praises. "Eh, dear!" my grandfather would say. "I don't know what there is for you to get aback of, youth! What do they learn you?" And I would try to counter, to show that I had some worth: "'Suomi' is Finland. On stamps. Grandad." "Yay, but what about the coefficient of expansion of brass?" said Joseph.

When I first went to Manchester Grammar School, having been entered for the exam by a perceptive teacher, my family was, in the abstract, delighted that I was going to "get an education", just as I might have been going to get a car. For them, it was a concrete object. None of us was prepared for its effect. That deep but narrow culture from which I came could not share my excitement over the wonders of the deponent verb. To them it was an attack on their values, an attempt to make them feel inferior. A shocking alienation resulted, which we could not resolve. Only my grandfather sat, and watched me; and listened. He said little, but at least he did not attack. Then, when he felt the time was ripe, he delivered his *coup de grâce*, from which, once heard, there is no retreat.

He uttered two precepts. They are absolutes. The first was: "Always take as long as the job tells you; because it'll be here when you're not, and you don't want folk saying, 'What fool made that codge?'."

The second was worse: "If the other feller can do it, let him."

* Solution p. 232.

That is: Seek until you find that within you that is your unique quality, and, having found it, pursue it to the exclusion of all else and without thought of cost.

It was staring me in the face. It was Robert's wall. On it was carved his banker mark, the rune Tyr, the boldest of the gods. When the Aesir went to bind Fenriswolf with the rope Gleipnir, which was made of the sound of a cat's footsteps, the beard of a woman, the roots of a mountain, the longings of a bear, the voices of fishes and the spittle of birds, Fenris would not allow himself to be bound unless one of the Aesir put his right hand in Fenris' mouth as a token of goodwill. Only Tyr was willing to do so. And when Fenris was bound, and helpless, he bit Tyr's hand off at the wrist, which is still called the wolf's joint. But had Robert known this? Was it a part of the Craft and Mystery of his trade? Or was it simply that an arrow is easy to carve? Yet he had got the proportions of it right; and we were all left-handed.

I loved Oxford, but it was not the wall. The wall was mine. Oxford was not mine. The rune was mine. It claimed me. Whatever it was that I was going to do with my life, it would have to be done here. This was my unique place. I owned it, and it owned me. There is no word in English to express the relationship. In Russian, the word is "*rodina*"; in German, "*Heimat*". And there, on the tree stump, by great-great-grandfather's rune and wall, I saw my "*rodina*", my "*Heimat*". This is what I must serve, as no one else could. This is the integration of my divided selves. Here is the site of the creative anger. Here I get aback of smith and stone-cutter and all of them. So, after a period of reflection, at three minutes past four o'clock on the afternoon of Tuesday, 4 September, 1956, I began to write a novel, *The Weirdstone of Brisingamen*, and I have been writing ever since.

One of the first things I discovered when I began was the esoteric meaning of "getting aback of". Whether it be building walls, mending kettles or writing a book, the activity is the same: it is the pursuit, through dedication, of the godhead. Such an indwelling calls for a clear understanding of what the nature of literature is and of what the story serves. The story that the writer must reveal is no less than the truth. And by "truth" I mean the fabrication through which reality may be the more clearly defined.

I live, at all times, for imaginative fiction; for ambivalence, not for instruction. When language serves dogma, then literature is lost. I live also, and only, for excellence. My care is not for the cult of egalitarian mediocrity that is sweeping the world today, wherein even the critics are no longer qualified to differentiate, but for literature, which you may notice I have not defined. I would say that, because of its essential ambivalence, "literature" is: words that provoke response; that invite the reader or listener to partake of the creative act. There can be no one meaning for a text. Even that of the writer is but an option.

Literature exists at every level of experience. It is inclusive, not exclusive. It embraces; it does not reduce, however simply it is expressed. The purpose of the storyteller is to relate the truth in a manner that is simple: to integrate without reduction; for it is rarely possible to declare the truth as it is, because the universe presents itself as a Mystery. We have to find parables; we have to tell stories to unriddle the world.

It is a paradox: yet one so important that I must restate it. The job of a storyteller is to speak the truth; but what we feel most deeply cannot be spoken in words. At this level only images connect. And so story becomes symbol; and symbol is myth.

I am using the word "myth" not as meaning "fiction" or "unhistorical", but as a complex of story that, for various reasons, human beings see as demonstrations of the inner cause of the universe and of human life. Myth is quite different from philosophy in the sense of abstract concepts. The form of myth is concrete always, yet it holds those qualities that demand of the human mind that it recognise a revelation of the function behind the world.

Revelation is not always the same as total understanding. It can be a request such as Oliver Cromwell offered to the General Assembly of the Church of Scotland in 1650: "I beseech you, in the bowels of Christ, think it possible that you may be mistaken." Myth is not an invitation to be cocky as to what the Holy Ghost may have in mind. "For my thoughts are not your thoughts, neither are your ways my ways, saith the Lord."

It is one of the main errors of historical and rational analysis to suppose that the "original form" of a myth can be separated from its miraculous elements. "Wonder is only the first glimpse of the start of philosophy," says Plato. Aristotle is more explicit: "The lover of myths, which are a compound of wonders, is, by his being in that very state, a lover of wisdom." Myth encapsulates the nearest approach to absolute truth that words can speak. The wall and the rune. If the young man on the tree stump is a Parzival, "to get aback of" is the Quest of the Grail.

The most searching examination in the world is a blank sheet of paper and no questions. But there is excitement. There is purest joy. Each book requires intense research in areas hitherto not perceived as being related, in which the writer may start off ignorant but must become expert.

With the novel I have just finished, Strandloper, I have had to be knowledgeable in, along with much else: the Celtic cult of the human head; the symbolism of English mediaeval stained glass; the thieves' language of Cant; the neurology of the human brain, especially in its relationship to the optic nerve; the survival of animism under the nose of the Church; the attitude towards literacy in the late eighteenth century as a result of the French Revolution; heraldry; Australian Aboriginal philosophy . . . It was ridiculous, absurd, then, but the excitement and the joy and the creativity occur at the point where those connected themes are seen, for the first time in the mind of man, to be one. And, at that point, the book waits. And the other feller couldn't do it.

Because of my nature, I find "spiritual" and "creative" to be synonymous. I am not exclusively a Christian; but, for me, work is prayer. So, in pleading for the nurture of creativity, in life and in education, I plead for the nature of the spiritual. I cannot separate the two. And, in this nurturing, I see particular aspects to challenge you; for the child needs your help if the creative element is to thrive. The first is that you will receive children to whom your culture is alien. For "Houghite", you may equally read "Shi'ite".

I can best illustrate this from personal anecdote. My maternal great-grandfather, William Jackson, worked at the same paper mill in Tamworth for seventy years. He died aged ninety-three in 1942 and I went to spend the summer with my grand-mother, his daughter. William Jackson was a Fabian, but his knowledge was that of an autodidact. For me, aged seven, the result was a treasure house, a magpie's library of unrelated books. And I was still bingeing. My great-grandfather had helped to found the Tamworth Co-operative Society, and had, through his long life, always been socially and mentally vigorous.* Therefore, in a hot July and August, I swallowed The History of the Co-operative Movement, Prolegomena to the Study of Greek Religion, Elements of the Fiscal Problem, The Golden Bough, Hone's Popular Works, the corpus of Thackeray and of Spenser, Carlyle, Swift, Dickens; British Battles at Sea, Nietzsche's Human All-too-Human, The Living Races of Mankind, The Works of Sir Thomas Malory, The South African and Transvaal War, Capital: from the German and Engel's Communist Manifesto of 1848.

Then I found myself in the middle of wonders: a Hindu epic poem of some forty-eight thousand lines, called Ramayana. Here were demons and gods and magic and talking animals and shape-shifters and mountain movers. Now I did not binge. I read. And, when I came to the final paragraph, I felt my heart stop.

* He was also an Equalized Independent Druid, but that's another story.

Thus ends *Ramayana*, revered by Brahma and made by Valmiki. He that hath no sons shall attain a son by reading even a single verse of Rama's lay. All sin is washed from those who read or hear it read. He who recites *Ramayana* should have rich gifts of cows and gold. Long shall he live who reads *Ramayana*, and shall be honoured, with his sons and grandsons, in this world and in Heaven.

So that's how he'd done it. William Jackson had read *Ramayana*. I could live to be ninety-three. But I had to look to myself. Sons and grandsons were cared for. No mention of great-grandsons. I'd better get going. "All sin is washed from those who read or hear it read." I could save the world. At least I could save Tamworth. I ran upstairs, opened the front bedroom window onto the street, sat on the sill, and, like some Hindu muezzin, summoned the people of Tamworth to hear Rama's lay. I went on till my voice cracked. And my grandmother, wise and wonderful woman, said nothing throughout my daily sustenance of me, Tamworth, world, and cosmos. For it was not time wasted. By repetition, I began to see patterns more than of gods with blue faces, flying monkeys, and many-headed demons. I saw, emotionally, more than one way to market. So, in our multiracial society, ought you.

The second aspect of creativity, which is the opposite of the first, is that you should be prepared for the effect of the education you offer on the background of the child. An immigrant family is an obvious area for circumspection, but just as explosive, and maybe more, is the middle-class English, when the child outgrows the family. How many books does the worldly man of affairs have in his house, and what is their tendency; and how is the child to convey to that parent that the universe may not be simply the sum of its material reserves, and success may not lie only in their exploitation for financial gain?

Thirdly, be on the look-out for overt, perhaps disruptive, creativity, and adapt yourselves to its needs rather than expect it to be moulded to fit existing preconceptions. There is your creativity, and it is your right: the bringing into being, new as a book, of the child's own spiritual nature, not the replication of others. Originality and individuality, in a trained mind, not corporate compliance will be essential to spiritual survival as Homo sapiens sapiens. For we are drifting, or being seduced, into another species: Homo inanis materialis.

Despite our daily observation to the contrary, I assure you that children are, by nature, spiritual beings, until we destroy through our example. In my own field of language I remember, and still can see, there being no problem here. A child knows, whether it be in the traditional structure of fairy tale, or the special use of an archaism, when the Mystery is engaged. "Once upon a time," or "Hear what comfortable words Our Saviour Christ saith," the child notes the cue and enters in. It is a truth that the Church itself seems to have lost sight of, along with much else.

I assert and would argue that we, child or adult, retain what comfortable words Our Saviour Christ saith, where our betters think we shall not.

> And He opened His mouth and taught them, saying, "Blessed are the poor in spirit: for theirs is the kingdom of Heaven. Blessed are they that mourn: for they shall be comforted. Blessed are the meek: for they shall inherit the earth."

Compare this.

> He began to address them. And this is the teaching He gave. "How blest are those who know their need of God; the kingdom of Heaven is theirs. How blest are the sorrowful; they shall find consolation. How blest are those of gentle spirit; they shall have the earth for their possession."

The former is literature written and translated by poets. The latter is tin-eared jargon by committee. The Beatitudes have been rendered *bêtise*.

In every language, literature, culture, of every time and place that I have met, the spiritual is set apart from the secular in some way, as a sign that we are entering a sacred space, a sacred time. It is done by one, or both, of two means: by ritual introduction and by a change of style, which is usually slightly out of date in grammar and syntax. And, at the finish, we are formally released into secular time and space. It can be a mere signal: "Once upon a time . . ." and "They lived happily ever after, until the Soviets came to power."

It can be epic. Vergil's *Aeneid*: "I sing of arms and a man . . .", closing with, ". . . but coldly droop the limbs, and, with a sigh, the soul, stripped of worth, slips out under shadow." Homer's *Iliad* begins with the invocation: "Sing, goddess, of the accursed rage of Peleus' son, Achilles . . .", and ends, twenty-four books later: "Thus they performed the funeral rites of Hector. There came an Amazon."

The *Odyssey*: "Tell me, Muse, of the man of many wanderings . . ." and finishes: "Pallas Athene, daughter of goat-skinned Zeus, appeared in the shape and voice of Mentor, and made peace again between the two sides."

The folkloric technique of entry and exit into and out of sacred time is used in the Bible, often to the delusion of commentators, especially those more inclined to fundamentalism.

St John's Gospel:

> In the beginning was the Word, and the Word was with
> God, and the Word was God.

"In the beginning" is, in New Testament Greek, "*en archē*", which is more the equivalent of "Once upon a time", not "At the Big Bang". And the Gospel ends with the traditional release: "If they should be written every one, I suppose that even the world itself could not contain the books that should be written."

It is not a Mediterranean ornament. In thirteenth-century Iceland, the one hundred and fifty-nine chapters of *Njal's Saga* begin: "There was man called Mord Fiddle, son of Sighvat the Red" and they reach their stark, formal close with: "And there I end the saga of the Burning of Njal." The sense of myth, even in history, is shown to be a special truth.

Often, especially in the preliterate societies, where every act tends to be linked to the spiritual, the whole structure changes at times of high ceremony. Among the Batak of north-east Sumatra, the men use a language that has no semantic links with their tribal, domestic speech, when they go out to fell camphor trees, which have a religious significance.

It is an example of what we appear to be losing: awareness of the risks inherent in the spiritual by its linking of timelessness with Time. It is a task for poets. Unless you know something of what others believe, it is not possible to appreciate the harmonics of your own belief.

For professional purposes, and out of an appalled fascination, I collect specimens of outstanding vacuity that try to replace the simple and the true. I rest my case on this, which I saw in a head-mistress' study, in beautiful calligraphy, framed, and hanging on the wall beneath a crucifix.

> The Lord is my Pace setter, I shall not rush.
> He makes me to stop for quiet intervals.
> He provides me with images of stillness which restore my
>   serenity.
> He leads me in ways of efficiency through calmness of mind,
> And His guidance is peace.
> Even though I have a great many things to accomplish each
>   day, I will not fret.

> For His presence is here,
>
> His timelessness. His all-importance will keep me in balance.
>
> He prepares refreshment and renewal in the midst of my
>   activity;
>
> By anointing my mind with His oils of tranquillity.
>
> My cup of joyous energy overflows.
>
> Truly harmony and effectiveness shall be the fruits of my
>   hours,
>
> For I shall walk in the Pace of my Lord
>
> And dwell in His House for ever.

There, in one clear example, is your spiritual obligation to literature: root out the reductive; seek excellence; pursue the numinous. And, along with a disciplined intellect (for one is no use without the other) give to the children their imaginations, their unique imaginations, of which they are being robbed with totalitarian intensity by the trash around them. I do not want to have sat on that cold tree stump in vain.

But the threat to the spiritual is not insular. It is global.

I first became aware of it twenty-five years ago, when my Japanese translator, Chozaburo Ashikawa, said to me that the Japanese world of business, men he called the new samurai, was intent on removing Japanese culture, and that the ethos was being built into the state system, so that in two generations the criterion would be success in trade. The Arts and non-applied Sciences were to disappear. Money and power were to be the goals. I could not accept the objectivity of his claim, until that Judas euphemism "vocational education" oozed into the language.

Now schools have begun to send me, instead of an enthusiastic or a questioning response to their reading, dour critiques of my novels couched in grotesque language, exercises designed to give the children practice in the writing of commercial English. The children are put up to this by teachers, themselves victims of traumatised ideologues of the Sixties and Seventies, and therefore not guaranteed to be coherent, to punctuate or to spell correctly, as their accompanying letters show. Truly, who will guard the guardians?

Should it not be a matter for gladness, for consolidation, rather than for criticism by the likes of cultural vandals and political levellers, that I, who grew up speaking the dialect of the Gawain poet, drinking beer in a smithy at the age of six, in a community that has a living Arthurian oral tradition, should also be able to save the good people of Tamworth, and, "while following with zeal his humble trade", to find out 'How-Mary-Gets-the-Eggs', to be able to come within an ace of demolishing my Officers' Mess, to draw on the wisdom of Racine, and Heine, and Pushkin, and Sappho, and Catullus, and Tacitus, and Thucydides, and Plato, and Wittgenstein, and Darwin and Jung; and to have read all Homer and Vergil; and to be able to set those wonders beside the wonders of quasars and quarks; and so to encompass the spectrum of our social and cultural diversities and to hand them on to the future not only as a spectrum, but as a rainbow and a religious, a creative, act?

Furthermore it is hard to find anyone who can understand the necessity for Latin in a Western society that has pretensions to civilised learning. There is a fine irony here. I spend time in Russia, where Latin has become a prized item of the syllabus.

Could it be that Russians have long realised that the way to understand a people and its culture is through its literature, which is why they are the world's best linguists? I know, from conversations, that they see our recent educational theories as barbarism, when it is considered more "relevant" to be able to order a gin and tonic in Frankfurt than to look into the heart of Goethe.

I am not immune. In my ninth year of a novel, my publisher and my agent suggested to me that I should abandon it, having spent enough to no purpose, and forsake "literature", and become instead a "popular" writer, cashing in on my established name by producing sequels to, and making series of, the earlier books on which that name was built. It is not "quality" now, but "commodity", that is in demand, the immaculate rubbish that we produce so well. No matter that it would render sterile the existing work, the life that produced it, and bring about my artistic and spiritual death. Houghites, R.I.P. Instead, I jettisoned publisher and agent.

The novel was finished in a little under twelve years. My grandfather would have found such statistics perhaps interesting, but irrelevant; as I do. The book exists. That is enough. From being a chaotic dance of the synapses, now it cannot be lost.

The novel is based on the true story of a Cheshire bricklayer of the eighteenth century, William Buckley, whom we should now call a Gifted Child, but who was transported for life to New Holland because of his precocity. He set off to walk home; met, and was received by, the oldest culture of the world, and one of the most sophisticated; adapted to it, and became a spiritual leader and healer, and then, after thirty-two years, he prevented a massacre of opportunistic, entrepreneurial Europeans that his People met, the contact with whom led to the People's physical extinction. But William could not express his wisdom except in a language that no Englishman considered worthy of learning.

Of the language of William Buckley's People, ninety words were recorded; yet they tell us much. Seventeen were the names of animals; seventeen the names of weapons; thirty-four, parts of the body; twenty, natural phenomena; two adverbial sentence modifiers: yes, no; three adjectives: good, bad, plenty; four verbs: eat, sleep, drink, walk; one imperative: hurry; one complete sentence: where are the niggers? And one answer: dead.

The single point of communication of this mix of philosopher, archbishop and Fellow of All Souls with the whites was the dialect of a twenty-year-old bricklayer. Is it the truth within such imagery, the myth, that attracted me, autobiographically, in the first place, that is now causing interest in the book, subconsciously, and the spiritual concern? Would *Elidor II*, *Owl Service III*, which the accountant-ridden publisher and agent were urging upon me, even if I would, or could, have written them, have caused so much as a flicker of an intelligent eyelid?

I find myself wondering whether my unschooled bricklayer is saying something of a more universal concern, which I was protected from seeing while writing his story. For the man was creative, was spiritual; and is now disturbing. He exemplifies what is beyond the reach of the swords of the new world samurai, that shifts and twists and dodges every fatal thrust: the mercurial Trickster of creativity. There are no stratagems, no guard against the illogic of the innovative leap. Creation is not in the Philistine accountant's vocabulary. He is the other feller, and he cannot do it. It confounds him. For creativity is risk. As the determination to walk home from New Holland was risk; and its reward a theophany.

I am not decrying the profession of accountancy, only its appropriation of competence in every field. And if, as it looms, we are entering on a period biased towards materialism at the expense of progress, then we are in the hands of the accountant, a spiritual Ice Age, where all will be frozen and there will be no risk, and, without risk, no movement, and, without movement, no seeking, and, without seeking, no future. Darkness will be upon the face of the deep. We must get aback of this.

Through creativity, spirituality, we shall; but it must be promoted, and given its head; which is the reason for my coming here today.

From my differing awareness, I sense something that you may not yet. Especially amongst artists (which is why, quite prudently, the Russians have always had the tendency to shoot us), resistance is growing. Consciousness is on the move. Something is at work in the world: a general recognition of a crisis of the spirit, of the banal and the shoddy, in human affairs. It is universal, and it must be met. Recently, an Australian Aboriginal shaman warned me:

"The Great Serpent has woken. Jarapiri stirs. The earth shakes. And the warriors are gathering."

And that's about the top and the bottom of it. The whole beggaring cheese. I've given you a story, not too long and not too short, just the length same as from you to me. I'd tell you more, gladly; but that's as much as I know.

3

Achilles in Altjira

I am here as the conscious result of events set in motion one day in October, 1950, by a remarkable man. Eric James, Lord James of Rusholme, was High Master of Manchester Grammar School throughout the seven years of my time there: a remarkable man; and a remarkable school, which instils the concept of excellence, in the absolute and for its own sake, within the individual, not the group; fitting the school to the boy, rather than making the boy conform to the school. In military terms: let a Winchester, or an Eton, be the Brigade of Guards. Then Manchester Grammar School is the SAS. Its planning of its mission (fulfilment of the boy's potential) is meticulous and humane: its execution ruthless. I have not yet reached excellence, but I was equipped by that school to seek it out.*

This may sound too close to a production line, and many of the school's detractors, who have not themselves been pupils there, disparage it as "Manchester Cramming Shop". But I have experienced what can happen.

One boy, gifted, articulate, acted at all times as if he were a steam-locomotive. He would chuff along the road and the school corridors, feet shuffling, cheeks puffing, arms working as pistons. When he reached the room where his next lesson would be taught, the door was held open for him, imaginary points were

* This lecture was delivered at the Children's Literature Association Tenth Annual Conference, entitled "Frontiers in Children's Literature" at the University of Alberta, Edmonton, on 15 May 1983.

changed to get him into the room and to his desk, and an imaginary turntable would turn him to be seated. Then the lesson began. At the end the process was reversed. No one mocked, showed impatience or criticised. He was accepted for the integrated totality of what he was. When, in his own time, that self-image changed, no comment was made, by staff or boys. Simply, the need for an aspect of being had passed.

That anecdote epitomised for me the greatness of the teaching at Manchester Grammar School: the ability to be perceptive, and the confidence to be eccentric. To this day, I am delighted to report, I know no member of the Common Room who is not a seeming loon. For therein lies the quality that sets the school apart. If the quest for excellence can be presumed, there is the freedom to be free. It is the most precious gift: a possession for ever. But what to make of that possession?

Eric James' contribution was that he, a Physical chemist, impressed on me, a Classical linguist, that without him Science might continue, but without me and my companions Western culture and the context and justification for his skills would be lost.

I remember the room, the window, the desk, the swirl of his gown as he turned and said to me (I was the boy in his line of sight, no more) that for each generation, the *Iliad* must be told anew. The moment is so clear because it was the first realisation that privilege is service before it is power; that humility is the requirement of pride. Without that realisation I should not have found the temerity proper to the will to write.

Today I want to discuss written language, as an art rather than as a science; and for the purpose of the discussion I shall take "art" to mean the fabrication whereby a reality may be the more clearly revealed and defined.

A prime material of art is paradox, in that paradox links two valid yet mutually exclusive systems that we need if we are to comprehend any reality; paradox links intuition and analytical thought. Paradox, the integration of the non-rational and logic, engages both emotion and intellect without committing outrage on either; and, for me, literature is justified only so long as it keeps a sense of paradox central to its form. Therefore I speak for imaginative writing, not for the didactic. When language serves dogma, then literature, denied the paradox, is lost. The steam-engine was a necessary part of one human being's development. If it had been quashed by dogma, the school would have survived; but would the boy? So it is if language is deemed to be the master of literature.

Two questions the writer has to answer before he can write are: What is the story and what words can tell it? The answers are the matter of my argument, and in order to achieve what the answers require, the writer must employ and combine two human qualities not commonly used together in harmony: a sense of the numinous, and a rational mind.

The revelation and definition of a reality by art is an act of translation. It is translation, by the agency of the writer and the instrument of story, across the gap between the reality and the reader.

The story is the medium through which the writer interprets the reality; but it is not the reality itself. The story is a symbol, which makes a unity of the elements, hitherto seen as separate, that combine uniquely in the writer's vision.

The words are the language: the means by which the story is made plain; and, unless the language is apt, the story will not translate, for the final translator is not the writer but the reader. To read also is to create.

Language shifts continually; it changes through space and through time. The problem is more easily understood when the language has to translate over chasms of space and time, for then the gap between story and reader, which is always present, is plainer to see. Eric James made me aware of the challenge when he said, "For each generation, the *Iliad* must be told anew."

Μῆνιν ἄειδε, θεά, Πηληϊάδεω Ἀχιλῆος
οὐλομένην, ἣ μυρί᾽ Ἀχαιοῖς ἄλγε᾽ ἔθηκε,
πολλὰς δ᾽ ἰφθίμους ψυχὰς Ἄϊδι προΐαψεν
ἡρώων, αὐτοὺς δὲ ἑλώρια τεῦχε κύνεσσιν
οἰωνοῖσί τε πᾶσι, Διὸς δ᾽ ἐτελείετο βουλή,
ἐξ οὗ δὴ τὰ πρῶτα διαστήτην ἐρίσαντε
Ἀτρεΐδης τε ἄναξ ἀνδρῶν καὶ δῖος Ἀχιλλεύς.

That is the opening of the Iliad as Homer told it. Clearly, we have to find other words. Here are some:

The Wrath of Peleus' Son, the direful Spring
Of all the Grecian Woes, o Goddess, sing!
That Wrath which hurl'd to Pluto's gloomy Reign
The Souls of mighty Chiefs untimely slain;
Whose Limbs unbury'd on the naked Shore
Devouring Dogs and hungry Vultures tore.
Since Great Achilles and Atrides strove,
Such was the Sov'reign Doom, and such the Will of Jove.

Thus Alexander Pope in the year 1715.

There we have an example of a generation's voice. But Pope exemplifies another theme of my argument: the duty of translation.

The more I contemplate the enormity of translation, the more I want to find some dark hole in which to die: or the more I marvel at the ingenuity of language. In this instance, the questions are: What is the essence of Homer? What is the unique, unmistakable genius, as opposed to the mechanical transposition of words? Words are more than the stuffing of a dictionary. They evoke mood as well as dispense fact.

My impression, when reading Plato, is that of drinking cold, fresh water. To me, Aeschylus is blood and darkness. And Homer is leather, oak, the secrets of the smith; Man; God; Fury; above all, magic and wonder in the world of Chaos and the logic of Dream.

I see little of that in Pope's immaculate couplets. His Iliad is the Iliad Homer might have written if he had been an English eighteenth-century gentleman of polite society. That is not quite the same as giving a generation its voice. The difference is important. Pope's duty was to translate to polite society of the eighteenth-century the heart and mind of Homer; and that he did not do. Instead, the Greek poet was dressed as an Englishman. I sometimes wonder what would have been the result if John Clare could have taken on the task.

Homer raises another issue that Pope illustrates by his failure. What is the writer to do when the text is not a written one? For where Pope wrote, Homer sang. His was an oral art, in which memory and improvisation were talents that are not used by the deliberate, self-examining, word-by-word progress of ink over paper. The word in the air is not the same word on the page. The storyteller meets the same problem now in a different guise: in the writing of dialogue, which is never mere transcription of a tape recording. This was brought home to me when I adapted my novel, Red Shift, for film. When the book was published, a frequent critical reaction was that it was not prose but a script. However, in the adaptation most of the dialogue had to be rewritten. What did several unnoticed jobs in the book, would not work for the camera.

So the chasm between literate Pope and preliterate Homer is valuable because we can see it. But the chasm is always there for every writer, too wide, and the translator's bridge too slender.

For the translator, the storyteller, there are the questions: what is the story and what words can tell it? We must add a question for ourselves: what does the story require of the teller? That is: what skills has the writer to deploy?

Since the purpose of language is to communicate, the writer must at least start from a shared ground with the reader. The place for worthwhile experiment to begin is in the middle of the mainstream. Linguistic and cultural crafts must be not so much simplified thereby

43

as embraced. It is not enough to know. It is not enough to feel. The disciplines of heart and head, emotion and intellect, must run true together: the heart, to remain open to the potential of our humanity; the head to control, select, focus and give form to the expression of that potential. A third necessity is that the writer should have authority: not the authority of a reputation, but the authority of experience. Without that experience, judgment is suspect, the necessary iconoclasm a mischief. In order to control the vision, the gift, the work, or whatever term we care to use, the writer is required to harness an untrammelled receptivity to a strict intellectual vigour. It is not necesary to be able to analyse what one is doing, as I am attempting now. Indeed, for some it may be inhibiting; but for others, such analysis is a positive knowledge, leading to a refinement of technique and thereby achievement.

Already we have a picture of a dynamic union of opposites: heart and head, emotion and intellect: not the one subservient to the other, but the two integrated. It is the tension of the paradox, and the paradox must be active within the writer. Yet when I look around I do not see it; and so, you may take this as a Black Paper of culture. I do fear for the decadent generation. I am not simply being middle aged. I am not blind to, or rejecting, new values. I am crying out against loss.

Let me make the questions personal: what is my story and what words can tell it? The words for me must be English words; and a strength of English is its ability to draw for enrichment on both Germanic and Romance vocabularies. The English themselves have no clear view of this. We tend to assume (because they come late in our infant learning) that words of Romance origin are intrinsically superior to those of Germanic. Certainly, when I look at my own Primary School essays, it is the use of the Romance word that has won for me the teacher's approving tick. But, in evolved English, the assumption is wrong. The two roots have become responsible for separate tasks.

We use the Germanic when we want to be direct, close, honest: such words as "love", "warm" "come", "go", "hate", "thank", "fear". The Romance words are used when we want to keep feeling at a distance, so that we may articulate with precision: "amity", "exacerbate", "propinquity", "evacuate", "obloquy", "gratitude", "presentiment". Romance, with its distancing effect and polysyllabic intricacies, can also conceal, so that the result is not ambivalence but opacity. Extreme cases are to be found in political and military gobbledygook, when Madison Avenue gets into bed with Death: Thus death itself is a "zero survivability situation", explosion is "energetic disassembly"; and we do not see human flesh in "maximise harrassment and interdiction" or "terminate with extreme prejudice".

Romance is rodent, nibbled on the lips. Germanic is resonant, from the belly. It is also simple, and, through its simplicity, ambivalent: once more the paradox.

A more general aspect of English is that vowels may be seen to represent emotion and consonants to represent thought. We are able to communicate our feelings in speech without consonants, and to understand a written statement when the vowels are omitted. The head defines the heart, and together they make the word.

A large vocabulary is another characteristic of English. English contains some 490,000 words, plus another 300,000 technical terms: more than three-quarters of a million fragments of Babel. Studies show that no one uses more than 60,000 words; that is, the most fluent English speakers use less than an eighth of the language. My own vocabulary is about 40,000 words: 7 per cent of what is available to me.

British children by the age of five use about 2,000 words; by the age of nine, 6,000 (or 8,000, if encouraged to read). By the age of twelve, the child will have a vocabulary of 12,000 words; which is that of half the adult population of all ages. 12,000 words: 2.4 per cent of the language is spoken by 75 per cent of the population.

They are rough figures, but even an approximation does not hide the discrepancy.

The purpose of language is to communicate. How can I, with a vocabulary three times bigger than that of three-quarters of my fellows, choose the words that we have in common? The question is unreal. I pose it in order to draw attention to the nature of imaginative writing. My experience over twenty-seven years is that richness of content varies inversely with complexity of language. The more simply I write, the more I can say. The more open the prose as the result of clarity, the more room there is for you the reader to bring something of yourself to the act of translating the story from my subjectivity to your own. It is here that reading becomes a creative act. The reason why I have no dilemma over choosing the one shared word in three is that the vocabulary I use in writing is almost identical to the 12,000 words of childhood and of most adults. They are the words of conversation rather than of intellectual debate; concrete rather than abstract; Germanic rather than Romance.

Through a preference for the simple and the ambivalent and the clear, the relatively sophisticated mind arrives at a choice of vocabulary that coincides with that of the relatively less sophisticated mind. It is in the deployment of the word that the difference and the sophistication lie. And, by deployment, by cunning, I am able to choose words in addition that are not shared and to place them without confusion and with implicit meaning, so that they are scarcely noticed, but the reader is enriched. It is a beauty of English. Yet I could be critical. English, for all its power, has mislaid its soul. English, despite my fluency, is not my own.

To make sense of what I mean, here is a little of my background, which is a background still common to many children in Britain today. I come from a line of working-class rural craftsmen in Cheshire, and was the first to benefit from the Education Act of 1944, which enabled me to go to the school with the highest academic standards in the country, and from there to Oxford University. Manchester Grammar School had at that time no English department. English, as a main subject, was for the few who could not master the literature of a foreign tongue. My ability lay in Latin and Greek. When I came to peer at English from the disdainful heights of the Acropolis, I saw only a verbal pulp. No writing, after *The Tempest*, had much to say to me. I was not surprised. Modern English, I would have said if I had thought about it, was a partial creole of Latin, and little more. My true discovery of English began some time after I had started to write.

I was reading, voluntarily, the text of *Sir Gawain and the Green Knight*; and I wondered why there were so many footnotes. My grandfather was an unlettered smith, but he would have not needed all these footnotes if a native speaker had read the poem to him aloud.

– a little on a lande · a lawe as hit were;
A balg berg bi a bonke · the brimme besyde,
Bi a fors of a flode · that ferked there.

This was no Latin creole. This was what I knew as "talking broad'. I had had my mouth washed out with carbolic soap for speaking that way when I was five years old. The Hopi, and other peoples, report the same treatment today.

Hit hade a hole on the ende · and on ayther syde,
And overgrowen with gresse · in glodes aywhere,
And al was holwe inwith · nobbut a cave,
Or a crevisse of an old cragge, · . . . .

Every generation needs its voice, but here was I, at home in the fourteenth century, and finding the English of later centuries comparatively alien, unrewarding.

"Yon's a grand bit of stuff," my father said when I read a passage to him, which he understood completely. "I recollect as Ozzie Leah were just the same." "And that's what all our clothing coupons went on, to get you your school uniform?" said my mother. Something had gone wrong. "Is there any more?" said my father.

I realised that I had been taught (if only by default) to suppress, and even to deride, my primary native tongue. Standard Received English had been imposed on me, and I had clung to it, so that I could be educated and could use that education. Gain had been bought with loss.

This sense of loss, I found later, had been expressed, albeit patronisingly, long before I could feel sorry for myself. Roger Wilbraham, a landed gentleman, read a paper before the Society of Antiquaries on 8 May 1817, in which he made a plea for what he called Provincial Glossaries. He said:

> "'Provincial Glossaries', accompanied by an explanation of the sense in which each of them still continues to be used in the districts to which they belong, would be of essential service in explaining many obscure terms in our early poets, the true meaning of which, although it may have puzzled and bewildered the most acute and learned of our Commentators, would perhaps be perfectly intelligible to a Cheshire clown."

Wilbraham was not wrong.

> "And I shal stonde him a strok · stif on this flet;
> Elles thou wil dight me the dom · to dele him an other, barlay,
>   And yet gif him respite,
>   A twelmonith and a day;"

In my copy of the text there is a note on the word "barlay": "an exclamation of obscure origin and meaning." But, where I live, it would take only one school playtime for that exclamation to lose all obscurity and to have a precise meaning, unless you wanted another black eye. It is a truce word among local children even now.

Years after my surprised reading of *Sir Gawain and the Green Knight*, Professor Ralph Elliott, Master of University House at the Australian National University, told me that I could be the first writer in 600 years to emerge from the same linguistic stock as the Gawain poet and to draw on the same landscape for its expression. Then I felt humbled, and, above all, responsible; responsible for both my dialects, and for their feeding. I saw, too, why little after *The Tempest* in English literature had said anything to me. It was an aspect of the Age of Reason that had committed the nuisance, and the nuisance was not only linguistic but social.

When the English, through Puritanism, tried to clarify their theology, they demystified the Church, and also cut themselves off from their national psyche; and a culture that wounds its psyche is in danger. The English disintegrated heart from head, and set about building a new order from materials foreign in space and time: the Classical Mediterranean. But, at the same time, they instinctively tried to grab back the supernatural. The supernatural was forbidden. It did not exist. That is the tension within *Hamlet*: "If only the silly boy hadn't gone on the battlements, none of this need have happened."

Just as I would claim that the English language benefits from the fact of having both Romance and Germanic roots, so I would claim that all language is fed from the roots that are social. But those roots were incidentally denied us by the sweep of the Puritan revolution. No distinction was made. Our folk memory was dubbed a heresy. The Ancient World was the pattern for men of letters, and the written word spoke in terms of that pattern. Education in the Humanities was education in Latin and Greek. English style came from the library, not from the land; and the effect, despite the Romantic Movement, has continued to this day.

Yet many British children share the experience of being born into one dialect and growing into another, and, since the Education Act of 1944, we have had an increased flow of ability from the working class into the Arts. The result has been singularly depressing. We discovered our riches, so long abused, and we abused them further by reacting against the precepts of discipline inherent in Classical Art as mindlessly as the Puritan revolution had suppressed our dreams.

Generally speaking, among the newly educated, the historical inability of the working class to invest time and effort without an immediate return has joined with the historical opportunism of the middle class and has produced a disdain for controlled and structured form. Excellence is not pursued. We are in a phase without direction, the heart ruling the head. It is most noticeable in theatre and in television, where surface brilliance is mistaken for substance, and verbal maundering is held to be reality. These are the wages of universal partial education. Now, to be cultured, it is enough to be vulgar. We are still reduced.

More sinister, this obscenity is creeping into all fields of expression by its gaining the trappings of propriety. The worst vandalisms are given the imprimatur of "Political Correctness". I know nothing of this phenomenon's rectitude, nor of its gubernation, but I see it more as "Ignorance and Uglification of English".

The whole rationale of what was happening to a great culture, which I have done no more than touch on here, was laid before me when I read *Sir Gawain and the Green Knight*. The irony was savage. I had been educated to articulate what that education had cost. But I was fortunate. I had a lifeline. I could get back.

The physical immobility of my family was the lifeline. My family is so rooted that it ignores social classification by others. On one square mile of Cheshire hillside, the Garners *are*. And this sense of fusion with a land rescued me.

The education that had made me a stranger to my own people, yet had shown me no acceptable alternative, did increase my understanding of that hill. The awareness of place that was my birthright was increased by the opening of my mind to the physical sciences and to the metaphors of stability and of change that were given by that hill. Until I came to terms with the paradox I was denied, and myself denied, the people. But those people had their analogue in the land, and towards that root I began to move the stem of the intellect grown hydroponically in the academic hothouse. The process has taken twenty-seven years, so far; and my writing is the result.

It is a writing prompted by a feeling of outrage personal, social, political and linguistic. Yet, if any of it were to show overtly on the page, it would defeat itself. My way is to tell stories.

It may be enlightening, or at least entertaining, to illustrate what I mean. My primary tongue, which I share with several million other people, a number greater than the population of Estonia, a country with a substantial literature, I would call North-West Mercian. My secondary tongue is Standard English, which is a dialect of the seat of power, London. Both are valid. Both can be described. Standard English, because of its dominance has the greater number of abstract words. North-West Mercian is the more concrete, with little of the Romance in its vocabulary, and native speakers think of it as "talking broad", and will not use it, out of a xenophobic pride and a sense of a last privacy, in the presence of social strangers. Social strangers treat it as a barbarism. There are differences between the dialects; but they are little more than differences. Neither is superior to the other.

In the sixteenth century, English achieved an elegance of Germanic and Romance integration that it has not recaptured. We respond instinctively to its excellence. The Bible had the good fortune to be translated into this excellence, and the debility of English thereafter is plotted in all subsequent failures to improve on that text. Here is a short passage from the King James' Bible and its equivalent in North-West Mercian, which I shall have to write in a phonetic abomination in order for it to be understood. But, spoken, it is poetry as is the other.

King James':

> And Boaz said unto her, "At mealtime come thou hither, and eat of the bread, and dip thy morsel in the vinegar." And she sat beside the reapers: and she reached out her parched corn, and she did eat, and was sufficed, and left.
>
> And when she had risen up to glean, Boaz commanded his young men, saying, "Let her glean among the sheaves and reproach her not:
>
> "And let fall some handfuls of purpose for her, and leave them, that she may glean them, and rebuke her not."
>
> So she gleaned in the field until even, and beat out that she had gleaned; and it was about an ephah of barley.

North-West Mercian:

> Un Boaz sed to ur, "Ut baggintaym, thay kum eyur, un av sum u' th' bread, un dip thi bit u' meet i' th' alliger." Un oo sit ursel dayn usayd u' th' reapers; un oo raut ur parcht kuurn, un oo et it, un ad ur filt, un went uwee.
>
> Un wen oo wuz gotten up fer t' songger, Boaz gy'en aurders t' iz yungg yooths, sez ay, "Lerrer songger reyt umungg th' kivvers, un dunner yay skuwl er.
>
> "Un let faw sum antlz u' purpus fer er, un leeuv sum fer er fer t' leeze um, un dunner sneep er."
>
> "So ur songgert in th' felt ter th' neet, un oo bumpt wor oo songgert, un it koom ter ubayt too mishur u' barley.

The language of *Sir Gawain and the Green Knight* is still spoken in the North-West of England today; but it has no voice in modern literature. The detriment works both ways. Modern literature does not feed from its soil. North-West Mercian is not illiterate, nor preliterate; it has been rendered non-literate and non-functional. I have just demonstrated its failure to communicate anything other than an emotion.

It would be retrogressive, a negation, if I were to try to impose North-West Mercian on the speakers of Standard English; and I should deservedly fail. Writer and language are involved in the process of history, and in history Standard English has become supreme over all regional dialects, of which North-West Mercian is but one. How then can I feed the two, to both of which I must own?

The answer is seen only with hindsight. Each step has appeared at the time to be simple expediency, in order to tell a story. One image, though, has remained: the awareness of standing between two cultures represented by two dialects: the concrete, direct culture from which I was removed and to which I could not return, even if I would; and the culture of abstract, conceptual thought, which had no root in me, but in which I have grown and which I cherish. It was self-awareness without self-pity, but full of violence. I knew that I had to hold on to that violence, and, somehow, by channelling them through me, make the negative energies positive.

All my writing has been fuelled by the instinctive drive to speak with a true and Northern voice integrated with the language of literary fluency, because I need both if I am to span my story. It was instinctive, not conscious, and I have only recently become aware enough to define the nuances.

First efforts were crude and embarrassing: a debased phonetic dialogue in the nineteenth-century manner. Such awkwardness gets in the way, translates nothing. Phonetic spelling condescends. Phonetic spelling is not good enough in its representation of the speakers. It is ugly to look at, bespattered with apostrophes, as my example from The Bible has shown.

It is the sign of a writer alienated from his subject and linguistically unschooled. Worst of all, in my writing and in that of others, the result, when incorporated in dialogue as an attempt to promote character, is to reduce demotic culture to a mockery; to render quaint, at best, the people we should serve. The novel, I would suggest, is not the place for phonetics.

Dialect vocabulary may be used to enrich a text, but it should be used sparingly, with the greatest precision, with accurate deployment, otherwise the balance is tipped through the absurd to the obscure. The art is to create the illusion of demotic rather than to reproduce it. The quality of North-West Mercian, as of all dialects, lies not in the individual words but in the cadence, in the music of it all.

So what words can tell my story? The words are the language, heart and head: a language at once idiosyncratic and universal, in the full growth of the disciplined mind, fed from a deep root. To employ one without the other is to be fluent with nothing to say; or to have everything to say, and no adequate means of saying it. Yet, for historical reasons, those are the alternatives for the artist in Britain today, unless he or she, consciously or unconsciously, wages total war, by which I mean total life, on the divisive forces within the individual and within society.

The conflict of the paradox must consume, but not destroy. It must be grasped until, leached of hurt, it is a clear and positive force, matched to an equal clarity of prose. It must be rage: rage *for*, not rage *against*. That way, although there is no guarantee, a new language may result that is neither false nor sentimental, that can stand without risk of degradation, without loss of ambivalence, and be at all times complete. Twenty-seven years have not given me that language, but at least I feel that I know some of its qualities, and where to look for them in myself.

Here is a tentative example, from *The Aimer Gate*. It describes, as did the earlier passage from the Bible, a harvest field:

> The men stood in a line, at the field edge, facing the hill,
> Ozzie on the outside, and began the swing. It was a slow
> swing, scythes and men like a big clock, back and to, back
> and to, against the hill they walked. They walked and swung,
> hips forward, letting the weight cut. It was as if they were

walking in a yellow water before them. Each blade came up in time with each blade, at Ozzie's march, for if they ever got out of time the blades would cut flesh and bone.

Behind each man the corn swarf lay like silk in the light of poppies. And the women gathered the swarf into sheaves, stacked sheaves into kivvers. Six sheaves stood to a kivver, and the kivvers must stand till the church bells had rung over them three times. Three weeks to harvest: but first was the getting.

Standard English and North-West Mercian are there combined in syntax, vocabulary and cadence. They speak for me, as the head to the heart; as the consonant to the vowel; as Romance to Germanic; as the stem to the root.

From such are the words formed. Now what else is the story? To answer that, I have to draw on the work of the late Professor Mircea Eliade, in whose precision of discourse I have often found my instincts to be defined.

The story that the writer must tell is no less than the truth. At the beginning, I took "art" to mean the fabrication whereby a reality may be the better revealed. I would equate "truth" with that same reality.

A true story is religious, as drama is religious. Any other fiction is didactic, instruction rather than revelation, and not what I am talking about. "Religious", too, is a quarrelsome word. For me, "religion" describes that area of human concern for, and involvement with, the question of our being within the cosmos. The concern and involvement are often stated through the imagery of a god, or gods, or ghosts, or ancestors; but not necessarily so. Therefore, I would consider humanism, and atheism to be religious activities.

The function of the storyteller is to relate the truth in a manner that is simple; for it is rarely possible to declare the truth as it is, because the universe presents itself as a Mystery. We have to find parables, we have to tell stories to unriddle the world. It is yet another paradox. Language, no matter how finely worked, will not speak the truth. What we feel most deeply we cannot say in words. At such levels only images connect; and hence story becomes symbol.

A symbol is not a replica of an objective fact. It is not responsive to reductive analytical rationalism. A symbol is always religious and always multivalent. It has the capacity to reveal several meanings simultaneously, the unity between which is not evident on the plane of experience. This capacity to reveal a multitude of united meanings has a consequence. The symbol can reveal a perspective in which diverse realities may be linked without reduction; so that the symbolism of the moon speaks to a unity between the lunar rhythms, water, women, death and resurrection, horses, ravens, madness, the weaver's craft and human destiny — which includes the Apollo space missions. All that is not an act of reason; but it is an act of story. Here is a dimension where paradox is resolved; for story itself is myth.

> In the beginning, the earth was a desolate plain, without hills or rivers, lying in darkness. The sun, the moon and the stars were still under the earth. Above was Mam-ngata, and beneath, in a waterhole, was Binbeal.
>
> Binbeal stirred. And the sun and the moon and the stars rose to Mam-ngata. Binbeal moved. And, with every movement, the world was made: hills, rivers and sea, and life was woken. And all this Binbeal did "*altijirana nambakala*", "from his own Dreaming"; that is, from his own Eternity.
>
> The life that Binbeal woke was eternal, but lacked form. This life became animals and men. And these, the Ancestors, were given shape and came onto the face of the new earth. And the place where each Ancestor came is sacred for ever.

That is a synthesis of a pan-Australian myth. From myth came the totemism of the Aboriginal Australian, and an awareness that amounts to symbiosis with the land. For the Australian, the Ancestor exists at the same time under the earth; in ritual objects; in places such as rocks, hills, springs, waterfalls; and as "spirit children" waiting between death and rebirth; and, most significantly, as the man in whom he is incarnate. It is a world view close to the one I discovered for myself, as a child of my family on Alderley Edge in Cheshire.

Through the mediation of myth, the Aboriginal Australian has not only a religious nobility of thought, but, coincident with the "real" earth, a mystical earth, a mystical geography, a mystical sequence of Time, a mystical history, and, through the individual, a mystical and personal responsibility for the universe.

Ritual initiation of the individual is the assumption by the individual of this knowledge and responsibility.

When an Aboriginal Australian boy is initiated into manhood, the sacred places of his People are visited, the sacred rites performed, to help the boy to remember. For this boy, this reincarnated Ancestor, has to recall the primordial time and his own most remote deeds. Through initiation, the novice discovers that he has been here already, in the Beginning, Altjira, the Dreaming. It is a Second Coming. It is a Holy Communion. To learn is to remember.

In Classical Greek the word is "*anamnesis*" and was first expounded to us by the father of Western philosophy, Plato. There are many differences between the Australian "altjira" and Greek "*anamnesis*", but both are a spiritual activity: philosophy for the Greek; life itself for the Australian.

I am not advocating a rejection of sophisticated values in favour of "primitive" animism. I am a rationalist, a product of the Classical Mediterranean, and an inheritor of two thousand five hundred years of Western thought. I need Manchester Grammar School just as much as I need Alderley Edge. But I do need them both.

My concern, in writing and in life, is that, by developing our greatness, the intellect, we should not lose the other greatness, our capacity to Dream. The two can work side by side, even if it means that I have to imagine a railway system to get me to my desk. Achilles can walk in Altjira. Indeed he must: he has such a lot to remember.

Not least of the memories is that to live as a human being is in itself a religious act.

That is why the stories must be told. It is why Eric James had such a catalytic effect upon one of his sixth-formers; and so justified his function as a chemist, after all.

4

A Bit More Practice

"When you've had a bit more practice, will you try to write a real book?"*

This frequent question is asked in the context of my having written four novels "for children", and, by now, there is a stock answer ready that seals off the conversation harmlessly, without bloodshed.

I do not write for children, but entirely for myself. Yet I do write for some children, and have done so from the beginning. This contradiction may be explained by two levels at which the brain works. Hindsight gives scope for rationalisation, but, at the time, the conscious motive for an action is crude and opportunist.

For this reason, any romantic picture of The Artist must be discarded straight away. I became an author through no burning ambition, but through a process of elimination, which lasted from the age of sixteen to twenty-one, rejecting everything until I had isolated the only occupation to offer what seemed necessary: complete physical and intellectual freedom from the tyranny of job, place, boss and time. The fact that ever since that decision I have worked a twenty-four-hour day, seven-day week, fifty-two-week year is a nice irony.

No publisher is interested in an unknown with nothing to show, nor is it common to find the sympathetic publisher and editor for a manuscript at the first attempt. I was lucky. Two years to write the book; one year to find the publisher; one year to publish. Four

* First published in *The Times Literary Supplement*, 6 June 1968.

years of dole queues and National Assistance. Some sharp lessons in human communication were learnt in this period, and one interview with the committee of the National Assistance board was so hilarious that it later provided material for a radio play. But "success" changes public attitude, and what was once called skiving, or irresponsibility, or failure to see reality, is now called integrity.

My first attempt, The Weirdstone of Brisingamen, is a fairly bad book, but there had to be a start somewhere, and consolation rests in the even worse first drafts of the opening chapter, which I pin up when things seem to be going well. Only recently have I come to realise that, when writing for myself, I am still writing for children; or, rather, for adolescents. By adolescence I mean an arbitrary age of somewhere between ten and eighteen. This group of people is the most important of all, and it makes the best audience. Few adults read with a comparable involvement. Yet I suspect that even here is not the true answer. In each of my books, the child protagonists have aged. The distance between them and me has stayed the same. Is that a coincidence, or have I been engaged in something much more subtle and unconscious, to do with my own psyche, not theirs?

But an argument can still be made that avoids such inner plunderings. The age of the individual does not necessarily relate to the maturity. Therefore, in order to connect, the book must be written for all levels of experience. This means that any given piece of text must work at simple plot level, so that the reader is compelled to turn the page, if only to find out what happens next; and it must also work for me, and for every stage of reader in between. My concern for the reader is slight, to say the least, but I am concerned not to be the agent of future illiteracy. Anything else that comes through is a bonus. An onion can be peeled down through its layers, but it is always at every layer an onion. I try to write onions.

The disciplines of poetry are called for to achieve validity at so many levels. Simplicity, pace, compression are needed, so that the reader who has not experienced what I am getting at will not be held up, since the same text is also fulfilling the demands of the plot. And my requirements are satisfied, because this discipline has made me reduce what I have to say to its purest form, communicating primarily with the emotions.

I make the first draft in longhand, because the elbow is the best editor, revise to the point of illegibility, and type out the result, some, but only a little, revision taking place on the typewriter. This first typescript is corrected, and, when it is as good as it can be made, a clean, second typescript is prepared, corrected, and sent to the publisher, who sends back a long editorial comment. Any second thoughts engendered by this are put into the typescript, and I consider the book finished. Corrections at the proof stage are almost entirely of compositor's errors.

The internal activities of a story's growth, however, are almost impossible to describe. Every book is the first: or ought to be. By this, I mean that any facility gained through experience should be outweighed by one's own critical development. The author should become harder to please. And not only is every book the first, by this definition, but no two books arrive through the same door. As a rough generalisation, there does seem to be a flexible pattern common to them all.

It is this. An isolated idea presents itself. It can come from anywhere: something that happens; something seen; something said. It can be an attitude, a colour, a sound in a particular context. I react to it, usually forget it; but it is filed away by my subconscious.

Later, and there is no saying how long that will be, another idea happens involuntarily, and a spark flies. The two ideas stand out clearly, and I know that they will be a book. The moment is always involuntary and instantaneous: a moment of particularly clear vision. The spark must be fed, and I begin to define the areas of research needed to arrive at the shape of what the story is going to be. It is an hallucination, but there is always the sense that the book exists already, has always existed, and the task is not invention but clarification. I must make the invisible object such that other people can see it. The period of research varies. It has never been less than a year, and the most, to date, three years. The spark struck by the primary ideas is all that originality is or can be, and the discovery of the point where hitherto unconnected themes meet is the excitement of writing.

As with all the books so far, *The Owl Service* contains elements of fantasy, drawing on non-Classical mythological themes. This is because the elements of myth work deeply and are powerful tools. Myth is not entertainment, but rather the crystallisation of experience, and, far from being escapist, fantasy is an intensification of reality. When I first read *Math vab Mathonwy*, it struck me as being such a modern story of the damage people do to each other, not through evil, but through the unhappy combination of circumstance that throws otherwise harmless personalities together. So far, and for about three years, no more than that.

Then I happened to see a dinner service that was decorated with an abstract floral pattern. The owner had toyed with the pattern, and had found, by tracing it, and by moving the components around so that they fitted into one another, the model of an owl could be made. The spark flew.

Welsh geology (I always start from first principles); Welsh political and economic history; Welsh law; these were the main areas. Nothing may show in the book, but I feel compelled to know everything before I can move. It is a weakness, not a strength.

I learnt Welsh in order not to use it. Through the language it is possible to read the mind of a people; but just as important seemed the avoidance of the superficial in characterisation: the "Come you by here, bach" school of writing. Presented with such a sentence, we know that the speaker is Welsh. We may guess that the author knows Welsh, especially if, from time to time, a gratuitous, and untranslated, line of the language is inserted. We can admire the author's erudition, or be irritated by it, but we do not experience what it is to be Welsh. This is "reality" laid on with a trowel, and it remains external and false.

By learning the language I hoped to discover how a character would feel and think, and hence, react. The importance is not to know that someone is Welsh ("*Diolch yn fawr*, I'm sure," said Williams the Post) but to experience the relevance of the fact. The success or failure of *The Owl Service* here is impossible for me to judge, but I am warmed to learn that the publisher has been approached to negotiate the Welsh translation rights of the book.

On a more general level: the ideas have struck a spark, and the spark has been fed. There is nothing else to be done but to write. At this stage, panic sets in, because the ground has been covered, and there just is no story.

Coming to terms with this has been difficult. I call it the "Oh-my-God" bit. I find myself unable to function at any but the lowest levels. The days are spent asleep, or reading pulp novels, and the evenings to the worst of television. Then a sudden, unpredictable, brilliantly original idea erupts, which makes me race around for a while, prophesying a great future. And then I remember where the idea came from. It is an amalgam of that book, and that film, and that conversation, and that book, and those notes, and that book, and that book . . .

There follows a string of such unexpected flashes of worked-out ideas, which have to undergo another process of shaping and selection, but this part is relatively straightforward, and it is possible to get on with the excitement of telling the story. The worked-out ideas form stepping-stones over which the book must travel with a simple logic. The details are never planned, but grow from day to day, which helps to overcome the deadly manual labour as well as to give the whole an organic development.

This has been, of course, no more than a statement of intent, since all books fall short of the vision, and the original question is truer than the questioner knows. There is always the hope that I shall write a real book: when I've had a bit more practice.

5

Oral History & Applied Archaeology
in East Cheshire

The purpose of this paper is to show how, in at least one instance, an orally inherited legend may give valid clues to the interpretation of an archaeological site.*

The legend I shall use is the Legend of Alderley. I absorbed it from my paternal grandfather, Joseph Garner, who was born in 1875. He lived all his life in the same house on Alderley Edge, as had at least the two generations before him. The Garner name occurs in the same square mile, the Hough, as early as 1592, and is one of the five basic families of craftsmen of the Edge, the self-styled Houghites.

> "Long ago, one day at the end of October, a farmer from Mobberley was riding to Macclesfield Fair. By dawn, he had reached Thieves' Hole on Alderley Edge. The horse he was riding was a milk-white mare, and he intended to sell her that day at Macclesfield.
>
> "But, at Thieves' Hole, the mare stood still and would not move. The farmer saw an old man, holding a staff, at the side of the road. The old man said that he wanted to buy the horse, but the farmer thought that he would get a better price at the Fair and he refused to sell.
>
> "The old man did not argue. He said that no one would buy the horse, and that he would wait for the farmer to return.

* This lecture was delivered at Manchester University on 10 December 1977.

"And so it happened. The farmer could not sell the horse, and the old man was waiting for him at Thieves' Hole that evening. This time, the farmer did agree to sell, and the old man led him from Thieves' Hole, by Seven Firs, and Golden Stone, to Stormy Point and Saddle Bole. He stopped at a rock on Saddle Bole and touched it with his staff. The rock opened, and behind it was a pair of iron gates and from them a tunnel went into the hill.

"The farmer was terrified, but the old man told him that there was nothing to fear, and led him down the tunnel into a cave beneath the Edge. Here slept a king, with one hundred and forty-nine knights in silver armour; and one hundred and forty-eight white horses. The farmer's horse was needed to complete the number of the enchanted Sleepers.

"The farmer was paid with treasure, taken back to the Iron Gates, and he found himself alone upon the hill. And though he often looked he could never find the place again."

That is the story as I remember it, told to me before I was five years old; that is, before 1939.

It is the myth of the Sleeping Hero, for which there are many analogues, in Britain and stretching across Europe deep into Russia. The hero is usually given the name of a national hero. In Switzerland, "he" is the three founders of the Swiss Federation. In the Devil's Den, on the Isle of Man, in Sutherland and on Alderley Edge, the Sleeper is nameless. There has been an attempt to call the Alderley Sleeper King Arthur, but I suspect that this was a nineteeth-century attempt at Romanticism. My grandfather had no name for him, and although he was literate, he did not read: certainly, he did not read treatises on folklore. Joseph Garner, whitesmith, of the Hough, knew only his sleeping king. He could not borrow from analogues. He had to tell the truth. We have here an oral tradition.

By the time that I could return to my grandfather with a mind trained and primed, my grandfather was dead, so I never could test the story in his presence. But I did have that story, and many of the analogues. If my grandfather had been word perfect, that is, if the actual words had been as important as my memory told me that they had been, and since he could tell only what he knew, it seemed to me that I had, within my own culture, a clue. I felt that there were answers to questions that I had not asked. So I set out to discover my grandfather's truth.

Let us keep in mind that the concern here is for archaeology, not for myth. It is the material culture of a people that I am looking for, not the numinous in Man. The numinous is present on Alderley Edge, but I am looking for the factual in a metaphor, and the first question is the hardest. It is that of where to begin.

The difference between legend and modern storytelling is that the modern story is a conscious fiction, whereas the legend, however degraded now, was, in its origin, an attempt to explain a reality. It is news that time has warped: a game of Chinese Whispers passed from generation to generation, so that what we receive now is a fantastic structure surrounding worn truth. It is a pearl. The shimmering accretions hide the central grit. How shall we look for the grit?

Francis Bacon knew the risk.

> "Now I suppose most people will think that I am but entertaining myself with a toy, and using much the same kind of licence in expounding the poets' fables which the poets themselves did in inventing them. . . . But that is not my meaning. Not but that I know very well what pliant stuff fable is made of, how freely it will follow any way you please to draw it, and how easily with a little dexterity and discourse of wit meanings which it was never meant to bear may plausibly be put upon it. . . . All this I have duly examined and weighed."

In other words, this time the words of Professor Cohen here in

Manchester: keep an open mind, but not so open that your brains drop out.

So I addressed myself to the Legend of Alderley. I began by accepting the whole legend as a literal truth about the physical Alderley Edge, as if it were history or journalism, all grit and no pearl, and from there examined it to see what could be ignored. The implication was swingeing. All elements for which there were analogues in other versions in other places were unlikely to be relevant to the Edge. It seemed that I could throw the story away and forget it. But Joseph Garner had told me something that mattered. So I looked again, differently.

I collected all the versions of the Legend of Alderley that I could find and compared them, not with those from other parts of Europe, but with each other. My comparisons, therefore, were with texts. And, at this stage, the analogues became significant. Superficially, there were wide variants, but there was a theme: that of a mortal becoming involved with an immortal through an intermediary. And the farmer always came from Mobberley, over Alderley Edge, at dawn on a day at the end of October, to sell a white horse at Macclesfield Fair.

A feature of oral, preliterate tradition is the importance of exactitude. But my texts were literary, of the nineteenth century, and their authors had felt neither inhibition nor an obligation to scholarship. Yet the source must have been oral, and I looked for some vestige of the tradition; and found one. Although the plot was frequently embroidered, a seemingly inconsequential detail remained constant, and was in the version told by my grandfather. For some reason, the route taken by the wizard and the farmer from where they met to where the Iron Gates opened was always given in the same words. "They went from Thieves' Hole, by Seven Firs, and Golden Stone, to Stormy Point and Saddle Bole." Though not proof, it was suggestive of an oral fragment, especially since only two of the places were still in living memory: Stormy Point (known commonly as the Devil's Grave) and Saddle Bole. The rest were lost.

Over a period of years I was able to recover the names. It was a slow matter of building up a series of fixes from documentary evidence, while taking none of the evidence for granted. Too often, authority for fact is based on the lazy multi-repetition of one unchecked error. The Golden Stone is an interesting example of a fix, and can stand for all. The oldest reference is from a Court Leet of Nether Alderley of 1598.*

> "On this day we did begin at the merestone at Findlow Hill and so to the great stone and so to the mere stone in the bottom of the ditch at the old dytche and so on up the old dytche to another merestone which many do remember stood on the end and is now fallen down, from there to a great mere stone in the Intack and straight to another in the bottom near the pit on the common that Lingard had marl out of and so lineally by the merestones to the top of the bank near Lingards house and so to a great stone called the golden stone on the north side of the main way that cometh from John Lingards to the Beacon."

Obviously the Golden Stone was a mere, or boundary, stone. By 1954, aged nineteen, I had enough fixes on paper to place the Golden Stone on the ground. And I went to the spot, and saw only an undisturbed bank of earth at the side of the track. I sat down and checked my fixes. They tallied. All that was missing was the Golden Stone. At which I waxed a little peevish and jabbed my trowel into the earth of the cop. The trowel blade snapped. I had hit rock.

A fortnight later, the Golden Stone lay excavated, and can still be seen. But the excavation was not all bliss. True, I had hit upon rock at the right place, but on the Edge it would be hard not to. For a day I was unimpressed by the systematic uncovering of a stretch

* A local court of record or appeal.

of Lower Keuper conglomerate sandstone, identical to the natural outcrops that surrounded the site.

Then patience, if not virtue, was rewarded. I came upon chisel marks and almost immediately a weathered, but definite, right-angled corner. The stone had been worked. It was not a rough outcrop. Eventually I found that it was not an outcrop at all. It was approximately 60 cubic feet of free-standing stone, the positioning of which had been important enough to cause the 4-ton block to be cut, moved and placed. Such was the Golden Stone: a grey conglomerate; not yellow, not golden. As with most discoveries, every solution asks more questions. Each place on the route was now known. I put them on the map, and looked again at the legend as fact.

The earliest written reference to the legend is in 1805, in the *Manchester Mail*, where it is stated that John Shrigley (who was curate of Alderley from 1753 to 1762 and died in 1776) held that the local peasantry believed the legend both to be historically true and to have occurred in about the year 1680; which is ninety years later than the first documented Garner in the district. Even at this naïve level of interpretation, my grandfather loses no ground. But let us accept John Shrigley's dates for the moment, and consider another matter.

The Edge was open common until the decade 1745–55, when it was afforested by Sir James and Sir Edward Stanley. Therefore, if we are to believe John Shrigley, the legend was current before the hill was wooded. Immediately the map is absurd. From Thieves' Hole to the rock known as the Iron Gates would, before 1745, have been a walk of 700 yards across open ground. But the route constantly referred to, "by Seven Firs and Golden Stone, to Stormy Point and Saddle Bole", is 850 yards, in a zig-zag line, that increases the journey by more than 20 per cent.

The phrase that had stood out to me as being an oral fragment made no sense on the ground. Yet it had been retained by the very people who knew that ground, as I knew it, as Joseph Garner knew it. Why was it so important that it had to be remembered? I went to look with fresh eyes. At each of those places I discovered singly, or in groups, hut circles, earthworks, tumuli, superficial pits and primitive hearths. The route of the legend made sense if it was seen as the preserved memory of a connecting path between a number of settlements. And here is the frustration of Alderley. The Edge is a public place, so heavily populated by visitors that any attempt at serious archaeological excavation would be to invite the destruction of the evidence.

In 1954 and 1955 I was able to make three small investigative probes, to try to establish whether there was a coeval pattern for the sites. The results cannot be said to be conclusive, but there is a prima facie case for considering the oral tradition of my grand-father to contain evidence of the Bronze Age. That is, I inherited a memory that was four thousand years old.

And here I would like to think aloud and to ask whether, if Arthur (or whoever he is) can survive preliterate tradition, he may also have swept similar fragments of grit into his synthetic pearl. The sword in the stone is a perfect image of the mystery of smelting metals.

But Joseph Garner is my concern here, and he has not yet finished with me. I am left with a grey Golden Stone.

The legend, by coincidence or not, had shown me a series of early occupation sites on the Edge; and I had seen them by trusting that the unschooled mind would convey information with less distortion than would the educated. I had believed in the belief of the storyteller, and found him most convincing when he had appeared to be at his most absurd. It was my introduction to the most valuable tool of any research: "Pursue the anomaly".

I looked again at the legend. It contained another absurdity: one that any fool could have spotted, but that this one had not. If we accept the legend as a factual report, the farmer must explain why he should be at Thieves' Hole at all. There is a road from Mobberley to Macclesfield, but it does not go past Thieves' Hole. There is even an alternative, which avoids the gradient of the Edge. The farmer was labouring, and off course. It was four years later, in 1959, that I saw. And it was one of those inductive acts of vision, the instant of clarity, that plagues years for its proving. My interpretation had been unintelligent. The legend was correct.

If the story has its roots in prehistory, "Macclesfield" was not necessarily the town, a paltry nine hundred years old: it could just as well be, in memory, the Forest, the land south of the Mersey, west of the Goyt, north of the Dane and east of the Edge. If that were so: and then came the intuitive flash.

In the boundary survey of 1598, we find a reference to "the Beacon". The Beacon, from my childhood, was a ruin on a mound on the highest part of the Edge. Before the trees were planted, it commanded a view for almost 360 degrees of an horizon that varied from eight to seventy miles in distance. But the mound is not contemporaneous with the building. It is a characteristic bell-barrow, from the surface of which I have frequently picked worked flint identical to that excavated more recently elsewhere in Cheshire, including the field next to my house, and assigned to the Bronze Age.

The Beacon does not occur in the Legend of Alderley, nor does it have any folklore of its own recognised by the old families. But it is an isolated habitat of the rare fern Moonwort (*Osmunda lunaria*), and that plant, though the Houghites do not know it, or have forgotten, has the alleged property of being able to draw the nails out of horseshoes.

It may not be irrelevant now to mention some of the foreign analogues of the Sleeping Hero. King Wenzel rides from his hill every night. Wild Edric rides as a portent of danger. Brian Boru rides round Curragh of Kildare every seven years on a horse with silver shoes half an inch thick; and, when the shoes are as thin as a cat's ear, the spell will be broken by a trumpet sounded by a miller's son with six fingers on each hand. At Cadbury, on the night of the full moon, Arthur rides with his men round the hill on horses shod with silver, and when they have ridden, they stop to water their horses at the Wishing Well.

We seem to have splinters of tradition here, where the Sleeper, the hill, horseshoes, silver and moon are linked. And, at Alderley, there is a well below the Beacon; but I shall return to that. For the moment, let me just stress that, although unconnected now with the Legend of Alderley, the Beacon has a force.

In 1959, I had been brooding over why the farmer from Mobberley should be riding a white horse over Alderley Edge on his way to Macclesfield Fair at dawn on a day at the end of October. And why was the Golden Stone grey? And what kind of beacon was the Beacon? I took the Ordnance Survey map and drew a straight line from the Beacon to the Golden Stone, 475 yards away. I projected the line in both directions. In one direction, the line passed through the centre of Mobberley; and, in the other, through the highest peak of Macclesfield Forest, Shining Tor, a crag of lustreless grit.

Shining. Beacon. Golden. Three words fortuitously connected with light. Mobberley, the Edge and Macclesfield could be linked. The farmer was in the right place at the right time: dawn on a day at the end of October. Along that line at Samhain, 1 November, the ancient beginning of winter and of the year, the sun rises, when viewed from the Beacon, over the Golden Stone and Shining Tor. And so does the moon at Lammas. Along that line, with a swing of only three degrees, the sun, when viewed from the Beacon, sets in Mobberley churchyard mound, marked by a glacial erratic boulder and a triangulation point, on May Day and at Lammas. Mobberley, the "moot-berg-ley", the "mound of the assembly".

A word about lines on paper. Many people seem to derive innocent pleasure from drawing straight lines in pencil across

Ordnance Survey maps. They claim that they are able to find align-ments, varying in number, over distances that are also not a matter of universally agreed lengths, between disparate, yet significant, features, usually four to each line, such as, *inter alia*: trig points, tumuli, crossroads, churches, erratic boulders and farm gateways. These lines, when "proven", are called "leys". The conclusions drawn about their meaning vary, but tend towards the arcane.

It is true that such lines can be found, which appear to pass through such objects. By the same process, however, it is possible to find that cinemas, post offices, filling stations, sewage works and, indeed, almost any feature one may choose, can be found to be connected by straight lines; but I have not yet come across any claims for their importance.

We should look at what is happening when a pencil is drawn across a map. Firstly, a map is a two-dimensional approximation to a curved surface. If we consider the most popular Ordnance Survey map, the 1:50,000 series, statistically, pure chance will give us fifteen hundred apparent optical alignments, and at least seventy-two will fulfil the requirement of "significance". But, to this, we have to add the width that the pencil mark represents. Even a sharp point makes a swathe approximately 17 yards wide.

We then must look at the conventional signs used on the map to indicate the features so precisely aligned by that swathe. A church-with-tower symbol covers an area on the map equal to about 50 by 45 yards on the ground. Clearly, no claim for precision of alignment can be made for such a conflation of potential for error. In the exquisite words of M. H. Moroney, those who seek truth by such means suffer from "delusions of accuracy". The only way to question whether there can be more than coincidence of error on the map is through the application of mathematics.* It is then that the smirk may be taken off the face of the archaeologist.

It does appear that the drawers of lines, in their *omnium gatherum*

* See Appendix on p. 242.

lack of discipline, have nevertheless discovered things of archaeological importance. A strong argument can be made for the existence of sky cults and of calendar markers that date from the Neolithic onwards almost accurate now and precisely accurate when erected.

Yet still there is need for caution. It is one thing to say that in prehistory Man could measure time from a given concurrence of data; but it does not show that in reality he did, or that he even felt the need. This quandary strikes close to home in both a figurative and a literal sense.

I live on a site that shows evidence of occupation in every archaeological period from the Mesolithic onwards. From the middle of a Neolithic circular earthwork, or complex of concentric earthworks, the observation of sunrise at the Equinoxes and possibly other calendrical events can be marked with precision. But this is not evidence that it ever was. With such caveats clearly stated, we can proceed with a more flexible mind and return to my own drawing of lines.

Why should the line from the Beacon miss Mobberley church? I checked backwards from Mobberley and found that the Edge obscured Shining Tor, so that the sun rose later, but from behind the Beacon, and that accounted for the three degrees. Yet there is something to add.

Archaeologists appear to have become afraid of speculation in this area, and I am not the one to blame them. On all sides, if they listen, they are threatened by Old Straight Tracks, blind springs, New Age mystics, dragon roads, and spacesuits. But I am not an archaeologist, so it does not matter if I make a fool of myself.

In archaeology, commonsensical explanations have not always taken entrenched positions. For example: it is useless to argue that if Neolithic man could do a, b, and c, why did he not do x, y, and z? Perhaps he did not want to. Or: that's impossible. It would have taken an enormous common effort and years of labour. Well, perhaps they wanted to. You and I may not wish to hack out the Golden Stone and to move it, but all that prevents us is our greater concern for other matters.

The pity is that idiots have driven a chariot of the gods through the greater wonders and the true mystery, and archaeologists have shut their minds, in self-defence, to all but the laboratory. One exception is Dr Euan MacKie.*

It is too soon to unravel the whole mystery at Alderley Edge. I shall confine myself to two lines of elucidation.

The first is that, about four thousand years ago, in the Bronze Age, there was a settlement of people on Alderley Edge. The second is that a structure existed for the measuring of time. These inferences are drawn as a result of my having examined an oral tradition, treating it as a literal report, and pursuing the anomalies, which I might not have noticed without an intimate and inherited knowledge of the place. What little there has been possible to examine on the ground has given positive results. And there are other intriguing questions: why are there iron gates? Why a hundred and forty-nine knights plus one? But I know very well what pliant stuff fable is made of, how freely it will follow any way you please to draw it, and how easily with a little dexterity and discourse of wit meanings which it was never meant to bear may plausibly be put upon it. So I thank Joseph Garner, whitesmith, of the Hough, for being true; and am grateful for what has come down through him, and leave it at that. Yet I should not be his grandson if I did leave it at that. I shall end by offering a few of my own observations.

The legend is the showpiece of Houghite oral tradition; but there are other, shorter, tales. Some 60 yards from the Beacon, and some hundred or so feet below it, is the Holy Well. It is a trough of four stone slabs under a cliff, with, next to the trough, a shallow quadrant cut into the bedrock. From this well have come dozens

* The author of many works, including The Megalith Builders.

of bent pins, now in the University Museum. My grandfather remembered the well as a cure for barren women. By my time, it had become a wishing well for weekend visitors, from which I collected my pocket money every Monday morning. And my children find it an irregular but still productive source of income. The only yew trees on the Edge grow there, and my grandfather remembered seeing rags tied to a dead hawthorn. He gave no explanation, and I was not curious enough to ask while he was alive. Below the well the ground is almost precipitous and is a deep bog, deep enough to strand a child. In it is a rock of unknown size, but of several hundred tons. It is reputed to have fallen from the cliff in the year 1740, and to have shaken all the cottages of the Hough.

There may be historical truth in this, for in the Court Leet of 1598 it is called the "Hanging Stone", but in the Leet of 1763 the same spot is the "Holy Well". More to the point, it is said that the rock landed on an old woman and her cow, who are as a result presumably still there. I find it too remote a chance that at the one moment in geological time the Hanging Stone should detach itself an old woman and her cow should have been up to their respective thighs and udders in mud on a near-perpendicular slope. I do not doubt the story; only the literal origin.

Elsewhere on the Edge there are other romantic items. The Wishing Well, which is a few yards from the Holy Well; the Wizard's Well, complete with portrait carved in the rock and the inscription, "Drink of this and take thy fill for the water falls by the wizhards will". A stone circle, called the Druid Stones. These are the reputed work of my great-great-grandfather Robert Garner, stone-cutter, who was happy to oblige both the Stanley and the Trafford families in the provision of dreams. I must own to Robert, because, although his hand is obvious to the initiated, he could draw a false trail across Alderley Edge.

Better evidence for the ancient pedigree of the Edge occurs in a charter of John de Arderne to John, son of Edmund Fyton. It is undated, but a study of the witnesses' names suggests a period between 1230 and 1250. Here, the same boundary of the Court Leets is followed, and the area of the Iron Gates is called "Elfgrenhoks": "*ad Elfgrenhocks ascendo*". "Elfgrenhoks" means "the sandy ridge of the elves".

The charter also contains the words "Fytoune strystre": "*exinde ad Fytoune strystre*". And, in the 1763 Court Leet, we find "to an Angle called Fitton Chair". It is another stone.

So we have: – a legend containing place names that coincide with the possibility of Bronze Age remains; hints of an alignment of man-made, with natural, features for solar, and perhaps lunar, measurements; a mortal, riding the sacred white horse in a sacred place at a sacred time, "dawn on a day at the end of October", that is, Samhain, the divide between summer and winter; and the mortal is taken by an intermediary to witness a dead, dying, or dormant bright Hero waiting under the earth, and to whom the horse may be said to be sacrificed.

This same place on the Edge is called "the sandy ridge of the elves" in the thirteenth century; at which time the name would have been no superstition or ornament, but a supernatural recognition. Compare, too, the Devil's Grave 50 yards away. And, separated from the main story now, but inseparable on the ground, a Beacon set on a tumulus, and the story of a woman and a horned animal and death at a sacred well. The Edge is as full of significance and function and continuity as a cathedral. We see a kaleidoscope, but not a random one. There is a pattern.

A clearer understanding of the Edge may be found in Máire MacNeill's definitive work for the Irish Folklore Commission, *The Festival of Lughnasa* (Oxford, 1962), which is our Lammas, where the themes to be found at Alderley are visibly coherent: white horses, boundaries, beacons, hill-tops, caves, treasure, buried heroes, intermediaries, old women, cows, fertility wells, sacred trees, the

Devil associated in a place name, stone alignments, stone chairs, elves, the sun, the moon, and town fairs.

It is not that the list is arbitrary but that it is so selective. Time and again these elements cluster, as they do at Alderley. It is in its present manifestation a Celtic cosmos, not an English one. It is old, and it is alive. I inherited it from an old man who would not have had the patience to listen to me speak at such length. But if he had not made me listen to him, I should not be holding now this polished, immaculate, perforated stone axe, an insignia of power of the Middle Bronze Age, from the Golden Stone. Coincidence, error, fantasy or folklore: this is a reality. And for this I care.

6

Hard Cases

For those of my generation, the increasing number of adolecescent doctors has become a commonplace; policemen have been our juniors for almost as long; it is not the law or medicine by which we plot the years, but a more startling hallucination that marks our tally. Hitler is getting younger.*

Those newsreels, familiar for a lifetime, no longer show senescent mania, but a madman in the prime of life. It is a salutory lesson in coming to terms with age; and, having made one such adjustment, it is with relative equanimity that I can face the implications of having been a published writer for a quarter of a century.

Twenty-five years; and over and throughout that time, certain elements have been a sustained part of experience. One of them is a dialogue with the teaching profession, which has shown me that there can be differences between our respective attitudes to books; I admit to a bedevilment by the concept of children's literature and writing for children. It may be that an examination of a particular view of the relationship between writing and reading will resolve the matter.

The puzzle is created for me through the letters I have received and which fill four filing cabinets. Each letter annotates a one-to-one engagement between the reader and the author. It is not a balanced engagement; for the reader knows the author intimately, through the book, whereas the author knows the reader

* This lecture was delivered at a meeting of The National Association for the Teaching of English, Birmingham, on 13 June 1985.

fragmentarily, through the letter. But what the reader does not know, and what the author comes to realise with time, is that the reader is a part of a consistent pattern of reaction. What is revealed by the pattern could raise questions for you both general and particular, about your purpose and mine. To begin with, it may be helpful for me to outline something of the background, of the letters and of the writing that has prompted them.

When I realised that I had to commit myself to the task of making intelligible marks on blank paper, I was forced to ask what it was that I could write and to whom it would be of use or even of interest. I felt that, at the age of twenty-one, I was scarcely in a position to tell anybody twice my age how the world should be run; nor, I considered, had I seen anything, so far, of startling originality and worthy of record. What, then, had I to say? And who would listen? Twenty-one years, it began to appear with painful clarity, was not time enough to equip a novelist. The more I pondered this, the more unavoidable the implication grew: I was making a big mistake.

Then I had a thought. If I were to write flat out, to the limits of my ability and experience, perhaps the result would be of use, and say something new, to people not twice, but half, my age. It was plausible. I should write for children.

Some weeks later, I took a sheet of paper, and, thinking that the moment would be either of import or it would not, wrote: "4.03 p.m., Tuesday, 4 September, 1956. Page One Chapter One.

"Colin and Susan Whisterfield, ten-year-old twins, sat in the attic window and looked gloomily out over the dismal London roof-tops, watching the rain slide steadily and stickily past the window, as it had done for over a week. It was the most boring rain imaginable; there was no wind to fling it against the windows and make you feel extra safe and cosy by the fire as the drops rattle angrily against the glass; there were no huge, black cloud mountains to eat up the daylight and make you feel just a little uneasy, even though you are safely tucked away in the middle of the largest city in the world. The rain just fell slowly out of a dull, grey sky into dull, grey streets."

And so on, until, mercifully quickly, I felt ill, and gagged on the mess I was perpetrating and stopped. I had learnt the first lesson: the duty of the writer is to the text. To think of writing for an unidentified audience is to forgo the prime commitment to literature. Conscious writing "for children", or "for" any other limiting group, is ghetto writing and not at all related to what I was setting out to do. It was not until the first of several visits to Moscow that I saw what can happen under the full flowering of such a prose. The only difference was that, there, it was not called a ghetto but a Union of Writers.

My plausible structure had collapsed, and there was no other in sight to support me. Yet the story I had begun was, I found, still alive and working. It was called "The Weirdstone of Brisingamen", and it would not go away. I had to write it, for its own sake and mine; so I began again, and, this time without any consideration for any kind of audience.

It is often said that one has either to suppress or forgive a first book; and The Weirdstone of Brisingamen has the strengths and weakness of all first books; but it was as good as I could make it at the time, which is as much as a writer can ever do. When a book is finished, it has to be let go. And that is how it has been with every one. I have made it as good as I could and let it go. I have written for the book, and have left the readership to take care of itself.

It would be convenient if I could make that bald statement and leave it at that; but the twenty-five years have shown me a less simple truth.

Despite my protestations about ghetto writing, it would seem that what I write is read by young people, if left alone, with greater intelligence, willingness, sensitivity, understanding and attack than most adults are prepared to allow me. Why this should be, I have no idea. If I do, after all, speak more clearly to a group than to the whole, I feel that the reason must lie rather with my psychopathology than with literary criticism, and I should be unwise to press the matter further.

I have fewer letters from children than from adults, but it is not the numbers that count. It requires involvement, I would call it disturbance, to produce the energy needed to compose a letter. That involvement most commonly registers as marked approval, or as a more marked anger; but it is not always so simple.

Because a writer is exposed in a book, sometimes the reader presumes a familiarity that the writer can find hard to handle. Letters can be explicit cries for help, and the writer must learn to deal with them properly, for even the most grotesque is a response to the words that were written; and such response begets responsibility. Yet that reponsibility has to be defined in the writer's mind, otherwise that mind is at risk. The point of cut-off must be clear.

But does the writer have a responsibility to the reader? The primary responsibility is to the text. What the reader makes of the text is outside the writer's control.

Does the reader have a responsibility? In a sense, no. Having established the contract by buying the book, or by borrowing it from a library, what you do with the book is your concern, and I must not complain. You may use it as a doorstop, or to press flowers, or even to teach from, provided you do not expect me to make the book heavy with the door in mind, large enough for your favourite poppy, or more convenient for your syllabus or philosophy.

Both writer and reader have further duties, if they are to benefit from their experience. A book, properly written, is an invitation to the reader to enter: to join with the writer in a creative act: the act of reading. A novel, it has been said, is a mechanism for generating interpretations. If interpretation is limited to what the writer "meant", the creative opportunity has been missed. Each reading should be a unique meeting, leading to a new interpretation. Nor should the writer's duty end at the text.

Writing is solitary and isolate, but only in execution. I work alone, in an empty room; yet that work, though solitary, is not private. Somewhere, in another place and another time, which will become another here and another now, there will be a communication with another mind. My duty is first to the text, because the writer is, by writing, above all making a claim for excellence. In working the language, as a farmer works the land, we seek to strengthen it against abuse, to protect it against decay, to encourage it towards growth. We hope to leave the language the better for our writing; and that writing is achieved only in isolation. Yet, at the end, there is always somebody, an unknowable "you", whom I wish to reach. And, for that contact, I am responsible.

Because you are unknowable, because reading should be itself a creative act, I cannot predict your response; but equally, I cannot ignore it. Response does beget responsibility; and the question of where that should start and finish is the question that is asked in every letter and becomes the challenge of each reply.

"I am writing to you rather in desperation, as I don't know of anyone else who might know. I have been drawn to witchcraft for a number of years, but as yet have never succeeded in contacting a coven. I read some books of yours a year or two ago, and I remember deciding at the time that if you did not actually belong to a coven, you were at least au fait with the subject. I wonder if you could suggest a good way to contact a local coven. Since witches generally keep the business to themselves, they're rather hard to find, at least round here. I would be grateful if you could help. But even if you can't, thank you for some beautiful books.

Love . . ."

"I am writing to you to bring to your notice, if you have not already seen it, an article in the *Daily Telegraph* of March 3rd. This states that a Wilmslow policeman saw an object surrounded by an eerie glow, a hundred yards from his beat on the A34 just south of Wilmslow.

"The U.F.O. was then said to have streaked off in a south-westerly direction, which is, according to my rough calculations, with the aid of the maps in *The Weirdstone of Brisingamen*, in the general direction of the Devil's Grave and the Iron Gates!

"Do you think that this has any connection with the Legend of Alderley?"

"I don't know whether or not you are familiar with the 'theory' of R. R. Shaver, a welder from Pittsburgh, Pennsylvania, but it would seem that your first book, *The Weirdstone of Brisingamen*, and J.R.R. Tolkien's book, *The Lord of the Rings*, and many others deal roughly with the same subject. 'What has Shaver to do with the above books?' you may ask. Well, Mr Shaver once had published a 'science fiction' story. This was all published as 'science fiction', but Shaver, and many other people, not only say they agree with him, but say that it is a FACT! No publisher would publish the story unless it was labelled 'science fiction'. They feared it wouldn't sell if otherwise labelled. Now, in your book, and those of others dealing with underground 'civilizations', there are two rival factions, one evil, the other warring on evil. Is your book based on fact?

"If by any chance your book *is* based on fact would it be

possible for you to let me know how you came by such information? I repeat, it is possible that it could reveal the mystery of flying saucers. If the answer is in the negative, I am sorry to have troubled you."

"I have been besieged by college boys at Brighton Technical Institute. The word has been put round that I know of the Secret of the Third Race, and where are the entrances of these caves. One asked me, where was the city of Lorr, was it in England?

"Some of the boys have been potholing in Derbyshire. Flying discs have been seen hovering over Yorkshire moors and Derbyshire for several weeks. I have been contacting people through the students. One I traced in Wisbech, Cambridgeshire, a very elderly man who worked in coal-mines. He has a map and some very rare knowledge. I have written to him and he spends his time fishing in the canals near Wisbech. The locals call him the Professor and they bait him. He wrote me a very guarded note of where to meet him, fishing at Floods Ferry, March, Cambridgeshire, in the Middle Level Catchment Board area; he has some secrets to impart; but I would have to treat him to dinner; he drinks light wine but does not get drunk. One student gave him my address when he did a tour this year with his friends. The student says he has some maps of the caves in Derbyshire and some unusual knowledge of the green men who come from the bowels of the earth.

"I wrote and told him that as a Cambridgeshire man and a keen fisherman, could we have a Research talk; he responded that he would be pleased to meet me, a real Fenman. He would exchange the knowledge for certain knowledge of the Isle of Ely. I have not the fare to travel with and put up for one night. Could this be a lead, do you think? Is it worth it? If I could get a small loan for the journey for Research work, I would go. Things are very sticky in Brighton at the moment. I am under the doctor, so would be able to travel on convalescence for a day or two to see the maps. The old man has explored several miles of caverns and seen the green men, and talked with them in sign language. Also some pieces of, or fragments of stars from outer space found thousands of feet underground. He has sent me a sample of a strange object; I have loaned it to a college student for chemical tests; and a fossil called a Shepherd's Crown given by the green men to the gentleman; it's a small one, very rare. I now believe that we might have a lead,

Best wishes,

Bill the Caveman"

"Re your beautiful *Weirdtone*, are you at all interested in subsurface matters? Our club has collected quite a lot of fantastic information we would gladly share, e.g. a major who says he entered Speedwell cavern, Derbyshire, and found a network of tunnels known to Boadicea. We quite understand authors are not obsessively interested in what they write about, but you seem to have 'more than mortal knowledge'".

From the whole correspondence (which includes the formula for making interstellar fuel from sea water), I have been able to infer what this "more than mortal knowledge" is that I possess.

Some two million years ago, a colonizing party from Alpha Centauri landed on Earth and established a base under the ice of the South Pole. Since then, the Alpha Centaurians have been monitoring the development of human intelligence. A tunnel-system has been made in the Earth's crust connected to the base at the South Pole, and at various significant places, mainly in northern Europe, including

Alderley Edge, depots of equipment and resources have been set up against the day, now imminent, when homo sapiens will have reached a level of sophistication that can accommodate the greater wisdom that the Alpha Centaurians are prepared to reveal to us.

Culture shock is seen as such a danger that the Alpha Centaurians have decided to prepare us by feeding our collective unconscious with images of the forthcoming truth. Their way has been to enrol certain individuals, of whom I am one, to supply parables through the ages, and, now that the day is at hand, to prepare young minds for the coming revelation that they will live to see.

That, briefly, is the state of things at the moment. And, when all the material, from different, yet cohering, sources, is read together, it has a compulsion and a momentum of its own. The main flaw is that it is all news to me. I am not a missionary. I just tell stories; unless the Alpha Centaurians are being subtle with me beyond my knowledge.

However, this exchange, of which I have given only a part, provides one of the clearest examples of the unpredictability of the reader's response. For most of the time, one's ingenuity is not so severely tested.

"Dear Mr Garner,

I have read both your books, The Weirdstone of Brisingamen and The Moon of Gomrath. They are the best books I have ever read. They are lifelike and exciting. I have never read a book so quick, then straight on to The Moon of Gomrath. I have read them over and over and over again. So, Mr Garner, I hope you will write more books like this about Colin and Susan. Please could you inform me if you do write any more books, will you inform me so I could get them?

Your admirer,

Frank Brooks, age 14."

That letter, from an address in the backstreets of inner-city Manchester, is typical of the headlong enthusiasm children can show for a book, if the reading of it has not been shackled by an adult. For the writer, the most heartening response is the repetition of the reading. And with the willingness to read goes a level of comprehension that such a complete engagement alone seems to produce.

"I am at the moment reading *The Owl Service* for the fourth time, although I should really be working for my History and English 'A' levels! I simply can't leave it, even though I know exactly what is going to happen. When I read it, I was inspired to read *The Mabinogion*, which I think is a marvellous book. Are the characters in *The Owl Service* meant to coincide exactly with those in *The Mabinogion*? I'm always a bit puzzled by that, though that is not intended as a criticism. I wish, too, that I knew what happened after the end of the book, although the ending is so good that anything else would have been a perfect anti-climax.

"I have read your other three books several times, but I can't go on re-reading four books for ever. So when are you going to write another? The last was published five years ago. Have you given up writing, or is the next book going to be a masterpiece? I hope it will be."

"I am a thirteen-year-old student in Tasmania. I have read *The Weirdstone of Brisingamen*, *The Moon of Gomrath* and *Elidor* and enjoyed them immensely, but even that did not prepare me for *The Owl Service*. I have read this book twenty-seven times! Each time I read it, I enjoy it more.

"Every time, I find more symbolism. How long did it take to write it? Things I especially liked were the way you used dialogue most of the time, and the way Margaret never actually appears in the book, although she controls everything. I didn't realize that until the second time I read it.

"However, for me, one of the best things about your book is the way you never tell the reader anything; you only show us through what is said and through events. I really enjoy writing – don't panic! I'm not sending you something 'for you to have a look at, sir'".

"I am a sixteen-year-old Australian schoolgirl, J—— P——, greatly interested in European folklore, particularly English. But being both Australian and a schoolgirl, my interest exceeds my knowledge. I bought *The Weirdstone* when I was twelve, and began to do 'research' on the origins of the names. I have discovered many, but there are just as many about which I can find no information.

"Do you think you could answer the following formidable list of questions? Do not, if you have too many other demands on your time, but I would be grateful if you would. Here goes . . ."

And here went. The list was, in truth, formidable in its length and in its detail. It took me two days to answer the questions, but they implied such a close reading of the text that I could be no less thorough in my reply. Miss P. did not leave the matter there.

"About nine months ago I wrote to you with a catechism on *The Weirdstone of Brisingamen*. I am now following this up, thanks to your kind encouragement, with another on *The Moon of Gomrath*."

The second catechism followed, which was another day's work in the answering. Then the letter continued:

"It is, despite being a distinguished Matric Literature student, impossible for me to be coherent in praising. All I can say about *Gomrath* is: blood on a silver sword across a fire is its atmosphere as I see it.

"Forgive me if I talk about myself when I say I'm talking about *Gomrath*. Literary criticism's a funny thing when it's not criticising, and I have nothing to criticise, for it either has to say: 'lovely, beautiful, marvellous' or make poetic similes like I did. So I'm writing a book. Writing helps you to understand writing, and I appreciate more such scenes as Colin on Shining Tor now I have tried to do the same myself.

"Could you please tell me something about spells and magic manuscripts? Oh, how awful it is to live in Australia! You are so out of it as far as information goes. And I love information. I get almost as much pleasure from tracking down your sources as from reading your books. I am copying out the Elder Edda by hand, having done the Prose Edda. Bother Australia and being sixteen!"

That was the end of the correspondence. Three years went by; then I had a postcard from Australia, scrawled on by Miss P., to tell me that she was about to take up a place at the University of Reykjavik to read Icelandic Studies. Nothing before or since has made me feel more elated and justified in what I try to do. To be able to stimulate the imagination of a Frank Brooks, age 14, in the slums of Manchester, and to trigger the motivation of an Australian teenager to find out how to cross the world to achieve what she needs, and for her then to do it, is worth all. There are just as many letters that make less comfortable reading.

"I hope you don't mind me writing to you, but I am currently undertaking a small piece of research for a post-graduate course at Loughborough University. I am particularly interested in the selection of texts for the English literature 'O' levels, 'A' levels and even degree. It concerns me that exams might actually discourage creative thinking about literature.

"I wonder if you have any thoughts, or reactions, about

your material being used. As far as your novels are concerned, they never actually appeared on the exam syllabus I did, and I had read *The Owl Service*, *Elidor* and *The Weirdstone of Brisingamen* before being officially 'introduced' to them at school.

"After this introduction, I dropped any other of your works immediately: it was almost as if my recreational reading had been made 'respectable' by appearing on the school curriculum. I don't think mine was a unique experience, either.

"I have since returned to your novels, but something is missing from that original experience: perhaps the intensity of the reading. I know I seemed to wander across the literature-field indiscriminately, absorbing it like some sort of ever-dry sponge. I read your work now (and I don't think it's a fault of yours) and that 'willing suspension of disbelief' has gone.

"To be fair, my changed experience of reading your work is not a fault of the exam system. But I think I might have continued reading your novels if they had not emerged in the classroom.

"The conclusion I am coming to in my work is that maybe English literature is unsuitable as an exam subject. It does not 'test' reader-response, rather the reader's memory of teacher-response, the 'correct' interpretation of the book.

"I would value any thoughts you have on the subject."

Here is my reply:

"You have touched on a sore point. It's a matter I've had ambivalent feelings about for years. I didn't know that *The Owl Service* was being used for a GCE text; and there was a time when the news would have made me run amok.

"I fear I have to agree with your initial conclusion that

English literature is unsuitable as an examination subject.

"In my experience, you are right, it does not test the response of the reader so much as the reader's memory of the teacher's response. Also, with schoolchildren, as opposed to undergraduates, I think that analysis limits, rather than illumines, comprehension of a text.

"I go to considerable lengths in my writing to convey aspects of being that are, by their nature, not open to reductive, analytical rationalisation; and to see, as I do, their being made the less, by teachers, in order for them to 'make sense' plunges me into pessimism.

"When, as also happens, teachers instruct me to be more didactic, to tell rather than to show, so that my books may be the more easily taught, and, I suspect, the more easily marked, I find it hard to remain constructive in my reply.

"And yet. And yet. The evidence can't be ignored that some children have their minds and souls opened by teachers who have shared with them a passion for literature. What it comes to is that there are never enough teachers who are good enough. Those with fire in their belly ignite fire in the bellies of the children; and those without, quench any spark."

I stand by that reply. It is a fact that, of all the letters I get from children, the only depressing ones arrive from a school address.

"We are writing on behalf of form 1P. We think your book *Elidor* is a bit far fetched and should be for a younger generation. We thought the last bit with Findhorn was the best. This was because of the descriptions, which made a vivid picture in our minds. But the first couple of chapters weren't all that good. This was because it hadn't got into much of an adventure. Questions: 1) Where did you get the characters from? 2) Where did the idea of another world come from? 3) Do you enjoy writing books?"

This kind of letter makes me ask questions. What teaching has produced such a lacklustre and sloppy approach? What is the point of the letter? What am I expected to do about it?

I have yet to find answers; perhaps because there is no one to ask. It would be unfair if I were to press the children. Writing to me was patently not their idea. And the teacher is hiding behind them, and cannot be reached.

It would not matter if such letters were a rarity, but they are common. Either there are two or three representative signatories to a single letter, as in the one above, or every child is made to write separately. Repeated phrases, blackboard mantras, tell me what has been taken from the teacher's instruction, and inter-locking patterns of shared statements show who is sitting next to whom. Often there are corrections and ticks in red ink to demonstrate the spontaneity.

Year after year this goes on, with every book; and it is coldly interesting that, without the dates on the letters, it would be hard to put them in their right order. Nothing appears to be changing. One has to close the mind against the implications of what some, and I know that it is only some, teachers are contributing to our culture.

Here is the latest, and it is the worst. It withstands multiple reading, and with each reading any explanation of its being recedes from me. Now it is my turn to ask for help. It is different in that the children's contributions are accompanied by a signed letter from their teacher: immaculate, apart from its punctuation, in Business English, limned with educational jargon.

"Dear Mr Garner,

I am writing this letter on behalf of forms [X] and [Y] who have recently been studying your book ELIDOR in their English lessons.

"They completed many speaking and listening, reading

and writing activities based on the text and found your book very educational and enjoyable to read. The enjoyment experienced when reading the book meant that the pupils were well-motivated which resulted in a positive outcome in terms of the work they produced.

"Please find enclosed some of their letters which outline what the pupils thought of your book and how useful they found it in terms of their learning.

"Many thanks."

I have quoted that letter exactly, because I do not begin to understand what is going on here. The children wrote, and here are merely enough examples to show my bewilderment at the apparent conflict between the teacher's letter, and the response of the class. What is going on? Are they on the same planet as each other? I am accustomed to being criticised, but this was a cesspit dumped on my head, and I cannot see the point of the exercise for the teacher or the lesson for me.

I shall run them on, after each other, to try to give some of the effect. The children would be between thirteen and fourteen years old.

"I think that your story was very boring. There was not enough action in it and the plot had been used before. I didn't really have a favourite part except when the story had finally finished. You could have improved the book by not writing it at all. The Book did not make me want to read it from the start and certainly not from the finish."

"I think this book is boring but I don't like reading books anyway but I have read this book and I don't think it is any good. For starters when I looked at the book I thought it was called Alan Garner. As I was reading this book it started to bore there is nothing funny or interesting. It was a big mistake was reading this book. You should of read this book your self and see what you have gone wrong you should of put something funny in it."

"Your book is boring and there was not much action and when there was it was no good so you could put more action in it. You could not get in to the story at all because the plot had been used to meany times. In fact it was a mistake writeing the story."

"I am writing to tell you what I think of your book. Nobody wanted to know. The book didn't hold my interest at all and I can't say I have a least favourite part because I didn't like any of it. It would have been better to have jazzed it up a bit."

"Your book wasn't any good and the ending was Rubbish."

"I thought your book was very borring and there was no action and I would recomend it to people that don't like action. I would give it 3/10."

"The best part of your book was the End because I was glad the Story was finished because I didn't understand it. The worst part was the beginning, because I knew it would go on and on and there was no fun."

That's enough. I find the whole thing mesmeric; but you may be by now professionally distressed. The school is an ordinary Comprehensive. I have checked. But something is agley. Failure to connect does not have to be aggressive. I admire this next school, writing of *The Owl Service*.

"Hi, Alan! This letter is supposed to be 300 words, but I bet you get letters from my other classmates that are only 200. This is 27."

"I enjoyed reading your novel. I didn't quite understand the book that much, but it was a great read and I would like to have read it some other time."

"I liked the book. All the parts were interesting to listen to it when other people were reading it to you because I can't understand it when I am reading it myself."

"Hi. My name is Paul. Our English teacher made us read your novel *The Owl Service*. I think that if your book had been written in English more of my fellow students would have understood it."

The main drift, is towards a drear comprehension. A teacher, who is typical, alas, wrote:

"For the past three years I have taken *The Owl Service* with our CSE candidates, and I think, especially with the abler girls, it has been the most popular book on their English literature course. Here are the lines we are working on at present:

1) Try to read Alan Garner's other books, and write a few sentences about each.

6) In what ways does the poem 'The Stone Trees', by John Freeman, remind you of *The Owl Service*?

8) Answer the questions on the blackboard about *The Mabinogion*."

How am I to reply to such as these? I do not understand how I can contribute to what I see as an abuse of story, at which, by replying, I may be thought to connive.

Teachers are no doubt as varied as the rest of our species. What concerns me, is that they are, briefly, in a special position of power at a time when their pupils can be influenced for life. What can I do to protect the future from this young man? It would be easy to diagnose nervousness alone; but I get too many for that to be a transitory lapse of nerve and grammar.

"Dear Alan,

I am a student teacher, beginning my second teaching practice next term.

"So what?

"Well, my scheme of work for class 2 who I am taking for English is an investigation of you and your work. Using you as a springboard, I hope to motivate them sufficiently to write their own interesting and immaginative stories of the inexplicable.

"So what?

"I would like your help. If you can write the boys a letter of encouragement, we would be 'cock-a-hoop' and you will have won thirty-one more fans. If you would like to offer suggesstions I would be grateful. If you would like to write a book about me, I would be flattered.

"Hoping to hear from you."

It is easier for me to cope with Bill the Caveman than with letters such as these. The difficulties, however, seem to work both ways.

"To the Publisher.

Dear Sirs,

As Deputy Headmaster of the above School, I was greatly disturbed when a member of my Staff of this school, brought the book *The Owl Service* by Alan Garner to me, which had recently been bought on this current requisition. Please refer to Page 64 of this book. I strongly object to the phraseology of this page, and I quote, 'Welsh git'. We are members of an organized Society, and we are expected to set an example, but if this is supposed to be the Example we set, how can we hope for the future? I find it disturbing that you have published this book. How many more Primary books of this nature have been published? Are other schools, who suffer from the current inflation, having to put up with this kind of rubbish? Isn't it the job of your Editor to edit these books before publication? Why do you advertise these, amongst worthwhile books, in the Primary Sector?

"I hope that your attention will be drawn to this matter and something could be done about it, at the earliest opportunity. I wonder what the Press would do with this kind of satire. Looking forward to hearing from you in the immediate future."

What I find most disconcerting here is that someone who writes such prose, with all it suggests, should be qualified to hold a deputy-headship.

"Dear Sir,

I am headteacher of the above school and I would appreciate it if you would forward my letter to Alan Garner.

"It was with his earlier books in mind that I purchased *Red Shift*. However, having now read it for myself I feel I must protest at some of the words used, such as those on pages 18, 20, 46, 101 and 109. I feel the use of these words add nothing to the story, indeed, they can only cause distress to people such as myself.

"I am very disappointed that Alan Garner has found it necessary to be fashionable in his phraseology at the expense of young and impressionable minds.

"This book was obtained from the Yorkshire Purchasing Organisation, Wakefield, because I took, on past experience, the suitability of the story. Other heads or teachers may not have time to read the book and would naturally include it in their school library with, I feel, irreversible and damaging results.

"I would be very interested in your comments on the matter and hope in future that I may once again recommend Alan Garner books with complete confidence."

"Alan Garner books". I spoke earlier about ghetto writing. I wonder, here, whether ghetto reading may not be another danger.

> "Dear Mr Garner,
>
> As an English graduate teaching in a grammar school, I have often recommended your books to my pupils. I am therefore disappointed to find that *Red Shift* does not possess the literary excellence of your earlier work.
>
> "I thought *The Owl Service* was a very interesting book, with passages of great beauty, but even in that I noticed that slang and bad language were creeping in. If our pupils read this kind of English, they will begin to write it, and this we cannot risk.
>
> "Also, I am sure that some of our intelligent and literary third-formers will not be impressed by the emphasis on violence and a rather distasteful aspect of teenage sexuality found in *Red Shift*.
>
> "I can see, of course, that both Jan and Tom are victims of an inadequate home background, but I cannot see the necessity for the foul language or the sexual immorality. We know that some teenagers are like them, but we also know that others are strongly idealistic in spite of the so-called permissive society. Why not write for them and help keep them so? Also, why not use your exceptional ability as a writer to perpetuate beautiful English, which seems in grave danger of disappearing?
>
> "I shall look forward to your future books, and hope you will return to your previous high standard."

The sad aspect of that letter is that the teacher and I care with an equal passion for the same qualities in language. There is so little dividing us, but it is fundamental in its effect on our perceptions.

The problem is not just local. Here is a letter from the librarian of the Horace Ensign Intermediate School, California, to the library supplier in New York.

"A brother librarian finds himself confronted with an irate parent who insists your selection *Red Shift* should not be on the shelves of any library. He threatens to go to the school board and if necessary hire a lawyer to protest the book.

"What help, if any, can you give us? If we continue to subscribe to your service must we read every book in order to prevent another incident?"

The library supplier's response was impressive. He sent the librarian a welter of supportive literature to show that the forces represented by the irate parent should, and could, be resisted. It included a booklet entitled *What to Do when the Censor Comes*. *Red Shift* was not prosecuted.

It would be dispiriting if all adult, and adult-directed, response were as I have shown. It is a significant element of my daily experience, but, happily, the greater motivator of letters is enthusiasm, not stricture: an excitement of sharing; and it must be said that some of the most supportive and encouraging reactions come from teachers, to whom I have been, without apology, giving what I see to be some necessary stick.

So I shall end on a few of the high notes, the celebrations of the creative act of reading to which teachers offer their lives, for which writers and pupils are grateful. What follows is not about me, but about what we all share in and hope for. It does exist.

"*Red Shift* is a wonder full book, Tough and smoothly styled as a steel vault. Contents very valuable to all: me too: who want greater freedom of subject matter for Young Adults' Literature. Awesome applause."

"I hope you don't mind me writing to you. I know it's probably silly, but I just feel I want to say thank you. A 12-year-old and a 20-year-old thank you.

"I have just finished re-reading *The Owl Service* for about the tenth time since I first read it as a pre-Agatha Christie

12-year-old. And I'm still emotionally churned up by it as I was the first time.

"I think I understand it better now. I mean, I really didn't have a clue what was going on during my initial reading, other than the barest story outline. But it hit me so hard and so deeply that I have never classed it merely as a book.

"It is, to me, an absorbing emotional experience. I think of it as my book. In the same way that, while you don't know me, you understand me. You have written for me. Maybe that's why I've got the courage to write to you. I certainly don't make a habit of this.

"I am a third year student at Frankston's Teachers' College and am majoring in Children's Literature. We have selected one author to 'study in depth' this year. I selected you upon the basis of my *Owl Service* obsession, but have since read most of your other works.

"Do you know, I think my self-indulgent motives for choosing you to study are beginning to backfire on me. I'm having a great deal of trouble writing about your works, especially *The Owl Service*. It's too close to me. It has dragged an almost primitive response from me, which I can't put into words, and, what's more, don't want to. And, apart from that, I can't bear looking at it in terms of literary structure: plot, theme, symbolism, yuk. It's above that. It is a creation and I can't destroy it like that.

"I think I'm going to fail this assignment! I'm at the stage now of tearing up articles by respected critics that insist on looking at your work in these terms.

"Anyway, I've raved on enough, even though I still haven't managed to say what I really wanted to. Mainly because I don't now exactly what it is. I hope you know what it is. Thank you again . . ."

I hope she did not fail her assignment, because there is one teacher in the making who "knows" what books are.

"Your work is becoming known here in Australia, much to the delight of my friend and me. Last year your books were on the reading list for trainee teachers, and it was through discussing the symbolism in *Elidor* with my friend, who is doing teacher training as a mature age student, that we realized the amazingly hard work you put into the structure of your books. It is giving us the greatest pleasure imaginable to plumb the depths.

"*Red Shift* had us in raptures. At *last* here is a writer who seems to know what goes on in our minds as we change babies' nappies and wash the endless dishes. You say it all for us, and awaken our grey matter once more, so that we can actually put into use all the accumulated data from our reading on myths and legends, Plato, the Eleusinian Mysteries, Jung. Everything is called upon.

"You *must* go on writing for yourself. It is the only true *self* we can all share.

"Joan and I discussed whether or not to write to you, because we know you must get a lot of cranky letters, and we didn't want you to think we were taking your time over nothing. Over nothing?!! It seems to me that, no matter how a writer insulates himself from his critics, he must, somewhere deep down, get some pleasure from knowing that he has touched the heart and mind of a reader, that the message *got through*. This is the point of this letter. Thank you from us both."

It is letters such as this that break down the necessary isolation of the writer and create a sense of community: not community of flattery, but a community of caring, emotion and of vision shared. Always the letters are accompanied by a shyness that, one feels, came close to preventing the connection, but the need to speak won through, just as the book did, against all the doubts and fears that attended its creation.

They are letters that humble, give strength and generate a pride and gladness in one's craft. They are not the reason or justification for writing; they are not essential, but it does matter to know, from time to time, that the night spent by lamplight, after the day of searching for wood to make enough heat for a fire to write by, so long ago now, also fuelled the will to give a sixteen-year-old girl from Melbourne the endurance to find her way to Reykjavik, and forced diffident intelligences to say that the message did get through.

> "I'm a teacher, and, over the past six years or so I've introduced many of my pupils to your work and watched them being entertained, stimulated and puzzled by it, particularly *Red Shift*. It has provoked more awkward questions than your other books and has consequently taxed my powers as a literary critic.
>
> "I just want to say thank you for the pleasure your writing has given me; thank you for the imaginative challenges it has set me; thank you for the long evenings you know nothing about talking with friends about your work; thank you for the friends you have helped me to make.
>
> "Oh dear, this has turned into a fan letter. But there. It's odd: when you read a writer you feel you know him, and there's an odd illusion of intimacy. I'm writing to the writer. I apologise if this letter intrudes upon the man."

I hope that, in trying to give you a view from the other side of the experience of writing, I have been as tactful. I hope I have not unwarrantedly invaded privacies. And I hope I have not been destructive in anything I have said.

There are differences between us. It may be that the purely academic mind will always be wary of the eclectic, deeply ordered chaos of the maker, and that artists will always and instinctively resist the scholar's quest for the finite answer; so our attitudes to literature will not be the same. Yet through literature we share the same purpose.

Whether alone in the classroom, or alone in the study, we work, through books and language, towards the one end: to bring about the future. Though Hitler may be getting younger, the future is our common cause.

7

Inner Time

This essay describes a Western European's experience of a primitive catastrophic process, its cause and its resolution. What follows is, of necessity, subjective. Any value it may have lies in that subjectivity, and should be compared with other, objective accounts of the phenomenon, which are to be found in textbooks.*

For our purposes, the experience began in the late autumn of 1968, when I adapted my own novel, *The Owl Service*, for television.

Translation of words into pictures is never easy, but the malaise that *The Owl Service* produced was unexpected: a combination of fear and exhaustion. The degree of exhaustion was debilitating, but the quality of it was worse. It was the sensation of walking unknowingly up an increasing gradient. However, the scripts were finished, and we started to film on location in April, 1969, with a schedule of nine weeks.

There are few occupations more tedious than the making of a film. Weather, money and time conspire to defeat the enterprise. A day's labour shows only some unrelated minutes of acting. There is no sense of dramatic progression, or even of emotional development. It is, of course, interesting and demanding work, but only when seen on its own terms, which, philosophically, ignore our Western concepts of time and space. Yet I felt pain: a threat from no direction, and a threat with no shape.

After a month, I was each morning late for shooting. My

* This lecture was delivered at The Institute of Contemporary Arts, London, on the theme of "Science Fiction at Large", on 26 February 1975.

behaviour did not hold up the film, but it did undermine the director. Soon, after each take, I experienced nausea. Then I was actually sick. We were in Wales, and the other members of the crew were too busy to notice my use of the nearest boulder whenever the director shouted, "Cut!" The next sensation was paralysis, which never developed, and fury against the actors; which did. I could not, dared not, speak to them outside the formalities of rehearsal and shooting. "They" were menacing, and at the same time witless. Unhappily, one of the actors was an incompetent, and it is a tribute to the film crew that he lasted the course. But I was less professional. My unpunctuality, the nausea, the vomiting, the sense of threat: all these symptoms switched to one great symptom in the middle of a take that involved the actor.

A delicate climax of the story was being filmed, and the actor was genuinely not caring, genuinely fooling about, genuinely antagonising the cast, the director and the crew, and I genuinely went to kill him. I remember leaning against one of my vomitoria, a stone wall, and seeing the daylight go out, except for a clear line around the actor's head. An animal roared inside and outside me, and I moved; but the sound engineer stuck his microphone boom between my legs and flicked me into a puddle. "I know," he said as he lifted me up. "But wait till next week. We still need him. Then I'll help you."

By the next week I was incapable of serving the film. Everybody was kind, asking of me only when it was necessary, but I had let them down. My token visits to the location were an embarrassment. I could do everything except work. But the film was finished on time, despite me, and we could all go home. June the twenty-first. The longest day.

Friends diagnosed my behaviour as nervous fatigue: I ought to take a holiday: I should pull myself together: I ought to get away from it all. The advice was well meant: endless: useless. I could not get away from it all when "it-all" was me.

After a sleep of several twilit days, I entered a zombie stage. I could move about. Then I recovered, and went seemingly mad in less than three months.

The most frightening aspect of such behaviour is its logic for the one who is experiencing it. I was so eloquent in my unreason. But, as the world crashed, while there was still enough of me left in command, I got myself to a doctor and said that I probably needed psychiatric treatment. "Thank goodness you asked of your own accord," the doctor said.

Now I must appear to change the subject for a while, but the purpose is to clarify the subject beyond misrepresentation and misunderstanding, because what happened to me was something normal; yet it was superficially so close to the esoteric and to the occult that it could easily be misrepresented and misunderstood. And if "normal" should be thought to be too imprecise a word, let me define it as "that which is found to be common among a group or species".

Having parked me in the comparatively safe orbit of a doctor's surgery, I should like to consider more generally the context of this essay. We are meant to be discussing "Science Fiction". I use the phrase with reticence. "Science fiction" has the sound of a botched-up job, but what it describes is an aspect of the most important function of literature, the one to which we turn in our greatest stress; that is, the flow of myth.

Man is an animal that tests boundaries. He is a "mearcstapa", "boundarystrider", and the nature of myth is to help him to understand the boundaries, to cross them and to comprehend the new; so that, whenever Man reaches out, it is myth that supports him with a truth that is constant, although names and shapes may change. From within us, from our past, we find the future answered and the boundary met. It may well be asked why we hold the key to questions we do not yet know, from what space and what time the myth flows.

The Biblical, the Epic, the Romantic, the Gothic are all merestones, boundary markers, of their day and the pointers of ours. Three hundred years ago, the mystery was in the greenwood; last century, the nearest grave; now, the nearest galaxy. For those communities, such as the United States, which, for historical reasons, have not had time to find their myth, the mystery is a strange hompolodge of external violence, and suspicion of one's fellows, and of the alien: the paranormal is paranoiac. I am not xenophobic. It is that for our time America may be manifesting phenomena that all cultures have experienced, at one level or another.

America is a nation that has grown too quickly from a conglomeration of relatively small communities, who knew, in their homelands, where they were. Confronted with a sea journey beyond their comprehension, faced with a field, the prairie, beyond their comprehension, ending in mountains beyond their comprehension, the only defence was to react in a manner that created whimsy, not myth. They had to mock the land. From this came the art work of Walt Disney, which, despite its gloss of sentimentality, has a dark undertow. It has only to be contrasted with the animation vocabulary of Eastern European film for the point to be made. At present the Americans as a nation have not found their myth, because they have not come to terms with the land. They are still on its surface; they have not entered in. Eventually they will. But, until they do, until they are integrated, they will tend to embrace Biblical fundamentalism while ignorant of Hebrew, and be condemned, for their myth, to the obligatory car chase, the shoot-out, and the flying saucer. [A nation that, in 1997, boasts a "Christian Dinosaur Park", is in psychic disarray.]

What I want to state is my view that the term "science fiction" is shoddy and uneducated, not a new branch of story. Whether we call it the manifestation of the Jungian archetype, or the manifestation of certain human behavioural characteristics, I find in science fiction the record of Man's boundary treadings. And there will always be boundaries.

I am myself, by others, dubbed a writer of science fiction, and I have to mention my books. They have, so far, been set in the present. The first pair I had written by the age of twenty-seven. I have dismissed them before now, especially *The Weirdstone of Brisingamen*, but recent events have made me withdraw some of my harshness. If you look at the two books as science fiction in the way I have defined the subject, they are a mess: a Manichean over-simplicity: but the germ of possibly my whole life is there. It took until 1975, and the performance of an opera conceived by me, and for which I wrote the libretto, to isolate the central question of those first "boundary" books from the matrix of their self-indulgent texts.

The change came with the third book, *Elidor*. The fragmentary northern ballad of "Childe Roland and Burd Ellen" was given its relevancy in the slums of Manchester. By "relevancy" I mean that the myth chooses the form for its clearest expression at any given moment. In doing so, elements may be revealed and materials used that earlier versions obscured or did not need. For example, in describing working-class areas of the industrial north in the middle of the twentieth century, as I do in *Elidor*, I am writing no tract; but, if my reporting is accurate, it cannot be without socio-logical content. But it is not polemical or didactic writing, any more than the purpose of *Sir Gawain and the Green Knight* is to record the discomfort of sleeping rough in armour, in winter, in the fourteenth century.

The fourth novel, *The Owl Service*, is an expression of the myth found in the Welsh *Math vab Mathonwy*, and is only incidentally concerned with the plight of first-generation educated illegitimate Welsh males. I labour the point because I am forced to accept that some readers will not differentiate between form and content. It is almost as if they are afraid to see.

The title of the fifth novel, Red Shift, prepares one for what is coming, and perhaps too much so. It may sound fictionally more scientific than it is. The myth is another ballad, the story of Tamlain and Burd Janet and the Queen of Elfland.

The element common to all the books is my present-day activity within myth. The difference between that activity and what are usually called "retellings" is that the retellings are stuffed trophies on the wall, whereas I have to bring them back alive. It is a process not without risk.

It would be a mistake to call the activity plagiarism, or the bolstering of a weak imagination. I would go further, and say that the feeling is less that I choose a myth than that the myth chooses me; less that I write than that I am written.

It was from my inability to understand the process that I appeared to go mad, but what I hope to convey is another definition; not insanity, but the conscious awareness of a dimension that the Pitjantjatra of Central Western Australia call "Altjira", the word usually translated by the solecism "Dreamtime". That is the boundary I tread. And I trod it all the way to the doctor's surgery.

We are fortunate in the part of the country where I live to have one of the most efficient psychotherapists practising today. His name is Bill Wadsworth. The first meeting was the popular cartoonist's impression. I talked for more than two hours without interruption. Bill Wadsworth asked me one question. I answered it. And he went straight to the centre of pain and gave me the insight to absolve myself from it. It was a remarkable performance. We made an appointment for the following week.

Euphoria lasted, and I attended with another heap of self-indulgence to wallow in. But Bill would not let me start. This time, I had to listen to him. And he put back, and tightened, every clamp he had removed, except the injurious one that had brought me to him. Then he dismissed me in a neutral voice, which, in my confused state, sounded heartless. As soon as I was outside the building I vomited.

The next, and last, visit was a perfunctory chat, less than half an hour. He was monitoring. Then we shook hands, and I thanked him and said good-bye. "I never say good-bye," said Bill.

So far we have an impressive medical performance. I was thirty-five years old, and had been carrying a bomb in me for nearly twenty years, and the filming of The Owl Service had ignited the fuse. Bill Wadsworth had isolated it, and dealt with it, in less than four hours of clinical time. It was a performance impressive in execution, but not unknown to orthodox science. Yet even here there were oddities. One is that I had started to lose hold on the world during the making of the film of my own book. Writing the original text, which was four years' conscious work, had not affected me. Another oddity is that Bill Wadsworth, dealing with an unknown patient who was irrational and disturbed, asked only one question the first time we met. Bill Wadsworth's question has implications for us all, even the most sophisticated, but especially for any artist. The question was simple, but its implications are so great that I have had to make this two-fold approach, at the risk of overstatement, in order to link the personal to the universal relevancy. Bill had asked: "Was The Owl Service written in the past tense and the third person or in the present and the first?" It had been written in the past tense and the third person. Although there was a lot of dialogue, it was all observed, "he said" and "she said", safely at a distance.

The crucial point is that an author's characters are all to some degree autobiographical: and the time of a film or a play is Now; dangerous as it ever was. The distance has gone.

Textbooks have a name for the disturbance, but it is a term that has been hijacked and abused by popularisation and by misapplication and redefinition at the hands of tendentious factions, with whom I am anxious not to be associated, especially the Church of

Scientology and its gormless substitutes for thought. So I must restore to the term its original, philosophical definition before I can use it. The word is "engram".

In neuro-physiology, an engram is the term for a hypothetical change in the protoplasm of the neural tissue which is thought by some to account for the working of memory. It is a memory-trace, a permanent impression made by a stimulus or experience. Music and smell are frequent activators of an engram. We reconstitute whole events from a line of Mozart or the scent of a flower. Proust spent twenty-two years in bed as the result of an engram. Whatever we may think of his labours, they demonstrate the power and ruthless obsession of the phenomenon, if it exists.

Pyschiatry takes the matter further. The human brain is exposed to influence from its development to death. Every event of life is recorded and is available to us directly; or indirectly through dreams, hypnosis or drugs. The difference between the direct and the indirect access to our files is that we usually have to surrender control of ourselves if we use the indirect methods. Most pleasant or unhurtful experiences are put straight into their files, engrams labelled. It is the unpleasant experience that makes the threatening engram.

Here is a typical pattern of engram attack.

Something happens to us. We are hurt. We do not like being hurt. "It" hurts. The event takes place in outer time, which is four-dimensional, and we, the organism, must continue. So, like an oyster, we enclose the pain, but, unlike the oyster, we produce no pearl. We enclose the pain by "being sensible", "putting it behind us", "setting it down to experience", "forgetting all about it". Whatever euphemism we choose, the process is the same. We wrap the engram round with emotional energy. But the engram lives on, because the engram is a creature of inner time, and inner time is one-dimensional; or infinite. The view from outer time is not clear. All events seem to be present simultaneously: only our immediate needs give an apparent perspective. We can check the validity of this argument by calling to mind any two intensely remembered experiences. They will be emotionally contemporaneous, even though we know that the calendar separates them by years. Similarly, it is possible to reverse the calendar by comparing emotions that are not of equal strength. An analogy may help.

When we look at a starry sky, we see a group of configurations that seem to be equidistant from us and existing now. That is an "apparent perspective". We are looking at a complexity of times past, a sky of "it-was", all at different epochs, distances and intensities. Inner time creates such illusions, also.

The next step is a big one. Just as we are physically the result of our genetic inheritance, there are psychiatrists who see in the engram a genetic ability to transmit itself. You may say (and I *do*) that engram disorder is explicable within the subjective inner time of the individual existence, and that that is marvel enough.

The severity of a given engram attack is related to the co-existence in inner time with all associated engrams, and their combined force threatens us. For instance, we have all seen a cat that has been squashed on the road. We have seen many such. Let us suppose that on one particular day we have three new and equally distressing experiences, but that one of them is also associated with the squashing of a cat on the road. That event will hurt us more than the other two, because it will be drawing on the hurt of all the cats that are being held in a memory bank in inner time. To continue the previous analogy: the cats are a constellation of pain.

Psychiatrists who would take the matter further and say that we inherit genetically and engrammatically, maintain that we have built into us the experiences of our parents from their conception to our own, and that our parents have inherited likewise from our grandparents.

It is obvious that, within a few generations of compounded inner times, the number of engrams available will approach infinity, and, whether we call the result "inherited inner time", "the collective unconscious" or "patterns of general human behaviour", the day-to-day result is the same. My own experience of consciously dealing with what Bill Wadsworth called a destructive engram leaves me with an acceptance of whatever-it-is as a reality, and of its ability to activate all its harmonics in the apparent simultaneity of inner time. But, attractive as the theory is, I have no evidence for my potential memory of what Grandad said in 1894, nor of the number of cats he saw squashed.

My experience does show, however, that a writer of fiction, willy-nilly, plants encapsulated engrams in his characters, and that disorientation, leading to symptoms that resemble madness, can be induced when the engram is made present simultaneously in inner and outer time.

When I set out to assault the actor during the filming of *The Owl Service*, it was because I could not reconcile him and me on a Welsh mountain in 1969 with the memory-trace of me somewhere else in 1950. The inner time co-ordinates were identical, but they had been externalised to a here-and-now of waking nightmare. Inner time rules of simultaneity and one-dimensionalism had been projected on to a four-dimensional space-time. Which was absurd. Or I was.

Bill Wadsworth's skill lay in helping me (without drugs, hypnosis or even leading questions) to see the simplicity of the trap: that the printed word is safe where the spoken word is not. My all-but insanity, provoked by conditions that externalised my thoughts and memories, jumbled, as actors, so that I was seeing a reality that, for me, was close to schizophrenic illusion, was the spontaneous and ungoverned invasion of the outside world by inner time. Bill Wadsworth showed me how to restore myself to my own co-ordinates, to release the energy that had been locked around the engram for nearly twenty years, and, above all, not to be afraid of the process. That is important because whatever words we use to describe the process, I am left with myself as someone who is obliged to walk in Altjira, to be a vehicle of myth, to go voluntarily (and now knowingly) to inner time, and to come back increased instead of diminished, with more energy than less. And it is astonishing what can happen when our energies are not bound up defensively against engram attack.

Before we move on, Bill should be demystified. His talent is directness allied to an acute and compassionate mind. His treatment is painful because we make truth painful, and truth is the only way to discharge an engram.

The method is simple. He gets his patient to tell the pain, to tell the truth. It is often an anecdote from childhood or adolescence. He makes the patient speak always in the present tense. Not "I was standing in the garden," but, "I am standing in the garden." When the story is finished, he asks to be told again and again, always in the present tense, until either there is nothing new left to say, or something new takes its place: a deeper, connected engram. It is like lancing a boil, or a series of boils; because the obvious engram may not be the final engram but the first, cumulative, and thereby injurious, one. We may think that it is the tenth squashed cat that is hurting us, but it is more likely to be pain associated with the first.

And here I must insert a warning. The simplicity of the present tense is a delusion. It is Bill Wadsworth's skill that makes it appear simple. I am able to face fear in his presence and to take emotional risks with myself only because I know that he is equipped with a multiplicity of formal qualifications of the highest achievement and can step in with a sharp word, or a sharp needle, if we meet demons. No one should be seduced into foolhardy experiments by any superficial lure in the experiences I relate.

So far, I have spoken of the engram phenomenon only as a symptom that interferes with the health of the individual. But the positive side is equally available, though we tend not to draw on it. Primitive peoples do; and "primitive" is not the same as "unsophisticated".

Inner time may not exist as such. It may be a confusion on my part from many sources; but it is an empirical truth for me, from which I am led to believe that Man is evolving, through that inner time as well as through other time frames, towards awareness of a universe that is conscious rather than effete. And to be conscious is to be responsible: to be responsible is to act: to act is to move: for ever.

Up till now that is an account of a condition that is behind me. The intervening years have been filled with activity made possible by the discharge of a crippling engram, and here are some of the results.

Immediately "after" being treated clinically by Bill Wadsworth, I organised the dismantling, repair and re-erection of the most important timber-framed Tudor domestic building known to have survived; had it linked to the existing mediaeval longhouse where I live; filmed and photographed the operation, and handled the archaeological complexities involved. (The mediaeval hall-hovel is on a Saxon/Iron Age/Bronze Age/Neolithic/Mesolithic site.)

I wrote *Red Shift*; made a television documentary film; wrote a television play; conceived and wrote the libretti for two operas; collaborated on a picture book for children; wrote a dance drama; wrote a study of a Jungian archetype; got married again; fathered a child; am monitoring another pregnancy; am collaborating on an analysis of a Middle English poem; am preparing one of the operas for filming on television; and am gestating the next novel. I feel under-employed.

In the fourteen years of work before my collapse, I wrote four novels, and did sporadic radio and television jobs in order to eat. Surely it cannot be a coincidence that so much should happen as soon as the energy needed to sit on an engram for nearly twenty years was made available for more constructive, outwardly-turned activities.

And, because I have long maintained that war memoirs are not as truthful as dispatches from the front, I have set out to demonstrate, in the only way I know how, that there need not be anything too terrible about what still has to be called "mental illness" by writing this essay in the twelfth week of another crisis; one caused by an engram in the opera I was writing. The opera is itself an expression of engram resolution and the nature of inner time, and I am still reverberating.

I have just given a summary of the main activities that occupy me at present, and contrasted them with the aridity of what went before. You may find both states unhealthy and ludicrous. But we are individuals, and it is not in me to be equable. The choice is only of which whirlwinds to ride. Given that, I am told my work is richer now, less diffused, and that I am more tolerably domesticated. The involvement of an academically trained mind with a primitive catastrophic process (that is, the waking experience of Altjira, the *Illud Tempus* of anthropology) is not always pleasant, but it is never far from what C. S. Lewis calls "joy", and I would have it no other way.

Let me return to the opera. I have devoted a lot of space here to engrams, but I have not described the subjective experience of discharging one: the road back from zero. As with the filming of the novel, when the opera was about to go into rehearsal; that is, to get off the page, to take on flesh, to be real people outside my head, I began to apply my brakes in the form of psychosomatic malaise. My wife told me that I should see Bill, but I ignored the advice. After all, he was for the big stuff, not backache and migraine. And anyway, I was "busy". Then, one night, I shouted in my sleep: "I wrote the thing! I don't have to watch it!"

When I heard what had happened, I scrapped the argument for not needing help; but, before I could get to Bill, the brakes were jammed on. Everything that had ever ached, ached. Each preparation for the journey to London produced another batch of symptoms, until I woke to find myself locked. I could not get out of bed. Hysterical paralysis had taken all the pains away. That made me angry; angry enough to have myself hefted into a car to keep my appointment with Bill. But the session started with me in ridiculous contortion on the floor because of muscular spasm, and barely able to speak. Here is how it went. The dialogue is surreal, especially out of context, but you should remember that Bill and I had worked together, and accepted a shorthand vocabulary between us concerned with effectiveness rather than with elegance.

"Go to the pain," said Bill. "Go to where it hurts most, and say whatever it tells you."

The centre of the pain was my left thigh. I zoomed in like a camera lens, crashing for the black centre, using my will as a projectile. Just before the moment of impact, the blackness switched off, and I was watching myself, six years old, at home, during the war, being sick after eating the top half of a teacake covered with blackcurrant jam, and developing the first symptoms of what was later diagnosed as meningitis.

Engram One. I told the story over and over, in the present tense, until nothing was left that was unpleasant, except the teacake.

"Go to the most painful part of that experience, and say whatever it tells you."

Again the crash zoom lens: into the teacake. And immediately another picture, another associated memory, a deeper engram.

A peculiarity of this technique is that, instead of becoming more tedious with each repetition, the description is more vivid, visually and emotionally (and therefore more difficult and painful), until there is a sudden loss of intensity, and the engram is discharged: but it is not erased.

The engram makes no distinction between an actual experience (one that we could photograph and record objectively) and a dream. The more dream-engrams there are, the more painful the process and the sooner the resolution. Also, the engram prefers the emotional truth to the historical truth, so that it does not matter if one is "lying" in the sense of untruthful evidence before a court of law, since we are dealing with the subjective truth of the pain in order to free it here-and-now: we are not conducting an experiment to test the accuracy of human historical memory and its retention. But the usual pattern is to move from historical event to historical event, sometimes taking shortcuts through truth and remembered dreams. Puns are common, too. After two hours of the first session I walked out with a sore leg.

We chased engrams all that week, until I crash zoomed into the last of the series, and found myself, screaming, aged three, being carried from my first visit to a cinema. Nobody had told me what a cinema or a film were, and certainly nothing about the concept of an animated cartoon; and I was taken into the largest enclosed space I had ever seen, into a crowd of strangers, put on a seat, and the lights went out. Figures fifteen feet high moved and loomed over me. The film was Snow White; and I felt my sanity slipping until the moment when the Queen metamorphosed into the Witch. Then I screamed, and screamed, and could not stop. My mother called an usherette, to have me removed, and I was handed into the strange-smelling arms behind a bright beam that dazzled me. The arms hugged my squirming form, and carried me out, while my mother stayed to watch the rest of the film. The exit was at the foot of the screen, and I was being borne up towards that great and drooling hag, away from safety, pinioned by someone I could not see, and the Witch was laughing.

When we got home, I was thrashed, for making my mother "look a fool in public".

"Go to the most painful part of the experience."

"Waiting with Mummy after the film, at the bus stop, before we get home."

"Isn't it a funny old world?" said Bill. "What do you feel now?"

"I want to be in London, so they don't foul up the opera."

"You'll still have a pain in your leg," said Bill. "It's sciatica."

And it is sciatica. But if I swear at it, it goes. I can will it away. In another century, I should be casting out a devil.

Whatever terminology we use, it is a fact that, from my hysterical paralysis and fear of watching the opera being performed, to wanting to be rid of a psychotherapist because he was delaying my arrival at rehearsal, and all in five days, was an achievement.

It should be noticed that Bill Wadsworth called a temporary halt and sent me to confront the opera in performance as soon as I said that the most distressing part of the aspect of the *Snow White* engram was my standing at a bus stop, afraid of what had happened, afraid of the thrashing to come, and denied my mother's affection in the present. It was a one-dimensional point of fear.

And when I first met Bill, when the world was crashing, and the personal pain was greater and its social effect a near disaster, we isolated one engram and discharged it: but only one. One engram for the edge of collapse; five engrams for sciatica. But there is a connection, and it is reasonable.

The Owl Service was written largely from a subconscious need to understand why, at the age of fifteen, I had, without justification or desire, verbally savaged another human being. I had done it at a bus stop. That was the centre of pain that Bill Wadsworth invited me to, and from which he enabled me to absolve myself. "The bus stop" was the engram I had not been able to recognise or discharge on a Welsh mountain.

When I was seventeen, the tables were turned on me by someone else in a similar way, and out of that bewilderment came the need to write *Elidor*. It happened, of course, at a bus stop. Even the first books, *The Weirdstone of Brisingamen* and *The Moon of Gomrath*, have bus stops within them; and they are based on the myth that is expressed through the opera.

Let us be clear, and remember the squashed cats. Three equally painful experiences happen to me on the same day, but one involves the squashing of a cat; and, therefore, all the squashed cats of my inner time bleed; and, if the engram has a genetic ability to transmit itself, the cats of my grandsires bleed, too. I have no doubt that I behaved intolerably to many other human beings, and they to me: but I retain negatively and destructively only the bus stop experiences, because they had the additional charge upon them of my infant terror and the withholding of parental love; which made me too cruel, and then too vulnerable, in my turn. It's a funny old world only here-and-now. For inner time, what I have described is that infuriating word "normality".

It seems to me that one motivation for a writer could be the need to discharge engrams. If it were as easy as that, writers would end up as saints; but, fortunately, there are too many engrams and too little life; and it will do no good to look for engrams cold, because any you dig out will be bogus, and so will you. Which is why, at our first meeting, Bill went only as far as the pain took me. I imagine that he could have forced me to more bus stops, out of interest, but he is a sensitive man. He knew what those twenty years had done, and that I needed to make up for lost time, and that it would be soon enough to help me further when the next stage was reached. "I never say good-bye" was his signal to be remembered when the need came.

The discharge of an engram through writing may be an act of exorcism, but it is not confessional writing. If it succeeds, I am not giving the reader the burden of my engram, but I am, fortuitously, handing on the released, and thereby refined and untainted, energy. Again, I could not do it cold, or with a social mission: I am not Galahad: but it is astonishing (and humbling) to read my mail and to have people say simply, "Thank you", and then to realise that they have taken something beneficial from a process that had been released through me, so that my bad 1949 becomes an unknown person's good 1975.

The danger of hubris is clear, but it is countered by the certain belief that, if the process were to be abused or manipulated, I should be destroyed, and by the cosmic joke of my own work. For there is not one problem sweated out clinically with Bill Wadsworth that I had not already myself posited, examined and resolved earlier in a book.

I got to London for the opera through dealing with a conflict that is answered in detail by the last chapter of *The Owl Service*, which was written nine years earlier. However long a novel may occupy, living the truth of it takes longer.

The present exercise with Bill Wadsworth is all laid out in the opera. I can even see where I am now, what must be done, and what the result will be. But I do not yet know how to do it. To achieve that catharsis, I shall have to write. And what will that uncover? And what will it take to answer?

The answer already exists in myth. If I have made the engram phenomenon seem hard, it is because evolution is hard, and we must evolve. I believe that we are evolving towards a hyper-consciousness of the individual, and that one of the evolutionary processes is concerned with inner time, a potential we are made aware of by the action of myth. At certain times in life, especially in adolescence, the potential universe is open to our comprehension, and it is not the engram's fault if we decide to be blind to the light and call on darkness.

The engram is not harmful, unless we ignore it. I have described no mystery that is not of our own making, no fear that is outside us. In other cultures there would be no need for explanation. But we are not other cultures, and I have no wish to enter Altjira as a Pitjantjatra, but as a twentieth-century Western European, with all my cultural skills intact.

The analogy of a starry sky may help us finally to understand what I mean. The Pitjantjatra live in Australia, now; but technologically they are twenty thousand years in our past. Their ingenuity of survival in a desert where we should not last a day is a product of the application of Altjira, 'Illud Tempus', inner time, myth, to their environment. The numinous quality of Man is dominant in them. But take a tribal Pitjantjatra and expose him to our technology, and he dies. He is no longer tribal, he has no co-ordinates. An individual who can cross the Dead Centre of Australia naked, cannot cross Sydney alone. He hits skid row instead.

The simultaneity of the Pitjantjatra and ourselves is another "apparent perspective", like the sky, and is what makes genocides of missionaries.

Somewhere in those twenty thousand years we sacrificed the numinous for our other greatness, the intellect. The mistake has been to atrophy our dreams. For the Pitjantjatra, both are equal, both spectra of the same rainbow. My intellect entered inner time as unprepared as a Pitjantjatra entering Sydney. But I survived, and have returned the better equipped to work. For now I know that, whatever the work is, it comes through me, not from me, and brings with it a proper pride, a pride in craft, not the hubristic pride of creation.

And I have no choice but to serve work; not only with the numinous aspect of Man, for which I make this plea, but with the intellectual and analytical force that is our history, and by which we move thought through outer space and outer time to other minds. The boundaries are endless. But we each have our role. Perhaps the artist's job is to act as cartographer for all navigators, and I simply plot the maps of inner stars.

* * *

POSTSCRIPT

Bill Wadsworth has died since the above was written, and so I am freed from the ethical embargo on using his name. He was a most complex man: an honest rogue, in that he was a hedonist, overweight, fond of material comforts and of getting them, and he charged his patients what he knew to be his worth. During a clinical session, he was always calm, and scarcely moved, except to pass the box of paper tissues. He could hold a silence as long as an actor can. But, once the clinical engagement was over, he became physically hyperactive, chain-smoked with trembling hands, talked intellectual and metaphysical rubbish fast and long, as if it were necessary for his own sanity for him to spout garbage after two hours of the merciless and calm logic with which he had countered my hysterical outbursts of rant as I struggled in vain to get off his hook. He died, too young, of a heart attack.

He has been accused of being a villain. I don't know. What I do know is that, without his quality and agility of mind, his applied intelligence, harnessed to sympathy and empathy, I should not have survived. Moreover, after our first meeting, he did everything from then on free, never an account. When I questioned this, he smiled. An honest rogue, with dreams.

8

Potter Thompson

Potter Thompson lasts for ninety minutes in performance, and took seventeen years to prepare. I cannot say whether it is normal for a librettist to conceive and structure an opera, because I am musically illiterate. I know none of the technicalities. A score is a pattern, and C sharp or B flat are meaningless. Yet Gordon Crosse asked me to write for him, and *Potter Thompson* is the result.*

The seventeen years of preparation were spent in my learning something of the difficulties of language, and produced five novels and a Nativity play. By the time the fifth novel had developed, I knew that I had reached a point where the words were picked clean. I was at the bone. To have gone further would have been to snap syntax and to be in danger of writing a blank page. The next words would have to be inflected: they needed to be sung.

Crosse must have sensed this development before he wrote to me. We met, and he told me that the Finchley Group wanted to commission an opera, and that he hoped that Michael Elliott would direct it. For me, this triangular relationship has been an extraordinary period, after the essentially isolated time as a novelist. Director, composer and librettist were working together even before a theme for the opera had been chosen.

None of the three of us believes that much good can come of writing by committee, and *Potter Thompson* was not written in that way; but there was a collaborative aspect.

* This essay was first published in *Music and Musicians*, January 1975.

The best image I can think of is the three overlapping circles of the ATV testcard. Each is itself, different from the others, but, where they overlap, the colours fuse to white. That, metaphorically, is the area of collaboration, and it was my job to find it.

There were requirements dictated by the nature of the commission: professional standards, based on children's performances. We agreed that the piece should be immediately exciting, without loss of subtlety. I felt that a mythological root was needed, and I remember churning out myth after myth, while my collaborators shook their heads in a sustained display of non-collaboration. I was looking for the white overlap, and I was not succeeding.

Then I suggested the myth of the Sleeping Hero, a prime myth of Britain. My childhood had been spent on one of the sites of its manifestation, and it had generated my first book. It ought to have been my first thought for the opera, because, as soon as I mentioned it, we had our common ground.

The myth takes several forms, but the central story is of the man who finds the Hero asleep under a hill, starts to wake him, but stops short of the final ritual act. Our common ground was a curiosity to discover why the mortal refuses the immortal. Why does Potter Thompson not bring the shining Hero out of the hill?

To précis a work is to diminish it. To say what *Potter Thompson* is about is to limit your freedom as an audience; but, if I am to convey something of the alchemy of collaboration, I have to describe the material.

The opera begins with Potter Thompson sitting alone on the skyline of a hill. It is Bilberry Night of Lunacy Day: the old festival of harvest, now no more than a village romp.

> Spring for ploughing, sowing.
> Summer, strength, growing.
> Autumn ripeness corn and reaping.
> Winter eating!

> Harvest is here and hunger is over,
> The red hag is dead.
> Picking of bilberries, singing and dancing,
> Bilberry bracelet boy makes for girl.

The decadence is obvious. The event is as religious as a modern Rose Queen. The villagers try to involve Potter Thompson, but he will not be drawn. He snarls his aloofness.

> They think they know!
> It's Bilberry Night.
> They think it's all over.
> It's just beginning.
> Let them be merry and marry,
> They'll never have rest.
> While they are leaping,
> Winter is creeping.
> I'm knitting a vest.
> Harvest is here and summer is over.
> Night stretches.
> Knit one.

From this superficial conflict between a gang of villagers and a pessimistic recluse the action changes abruptly to something menacing.

Potter Thompson is seen to be not so much anti-social as frightened. His fear is the secret pain that Bilberry Night holds for him. Once, on this night, when he was younger, his "ceremony of innocence" was drowned. We are not told the details: they would probably appear insignificant: but the moment has become trapped within Potter Thompson, and he within the moment. The pain is so unbearable each Bilberry Night, so strong, that it is personified as the characters called Boy/Girl. They sing the first line of the opera.

> And on a green mountain there stands a
>   young man.

The threat of Boy/Girl and the villagers makes Potter Thompson try to run away. He falls on the rocks and down into the hill. Here, through a phantasmagoria, he undergoes a mystical ordeal of initiation into the elements of his craft: Earth, Water, Air and Fire; and beyond these to the Sleeping Hero.

For me, this development of the myth was the clearest instance of dictate's stimulating, rather than restricting, invention. One adult professional singer, Potter Thompson, moves through, and is moved by, the vitality of children. Around his strength, ebullience can play, and together make something serious and new.

An example is the treatment of the Air Elementals. I saw them as dervish mops from a carwash. They dry Potter Thompson after his ordeal by water, working in pairs, as rollers. Yet carwash mops also resemble African masks. Children know the nice balance between humour and fear.

The Elementals who plague Potter Thompson are really his tutors, instructing him in the litany:

> What moves Earth?
> Water.
> What moves Water?
> Air.
> What moves Air?
> Flame.
> What moves Flame?
> Time.

Release from each element is always towards something that appears to be worse, and Potter Thompson moves only because he is goaded by the pursuing songs of Boy/Girl.

Boy/Girl link the external world of the village, the private world of Potter Thompson and the mystical world of the Elementals. They stand between ritual and tradition, and their words are close to those of children's playground games.

BOY:	She said and she said
	And what did she say?
GIRL:	She said that she loved,
	But who did she love?
BOY:	Suppose she said she loved me.
GIRL:	She never said that, whatever she said.
BOY:	Oh yes, she said, and that's what she said.
GIRL:	All dressed in white.
BOY:	She's for another, and not for me.
	I thank you for your courtesy.
PT:	Bird on briar I told it to.
	No other one I dare.
GIRL:	The nightingale sings –
PT:	All my life, leave me not –
GIRL:	That all the wood rings –
PT:	Leave me not, leave me not –
GIRL:	She sings in her song –
PT:	All my life, leave me not –
GIRL:	That the night is too long.
PT:	Not leave alone.
	Take this load from me,
	Or else I am gone.
BOY:	I am so withered up with years,
	I can't be young again.

On the surface of the story, Boy/Girl hint at lost love in Potter Thompson's youth: a wound that was the cause of his isolation and of his craft as a potter. At first, their role may seem to be romantic and lyrical, but they are an aberration, a sickness within. They are Potter Thompson's prisoners and they torture him.

Boy/Girl drive Potter Thompson towards the Hero. Each step from element to element, Earth to Water to Air to Fire, is made to escape them, but the more Potter Thompson dares, the clearer Boy/Girl become. As he passes through the stages of his initiation, he is cleansed, there are fewer and fewer impurities in his clay and therefore fewer and fewer distractions from Boy/Girl, until, rather than face up to them, he enters the furnace of the sun to the Hero's cave.

> But they're not here.
> No Boy and no Girl.
> If He wakes,
> Will there be no more?
> Will there be
> Bilberry end?
> My head no more
> Rampicked by the stars,
> No more agait with dreams?

In the consummation of the opera, the question that Gordon Crosse, Michael Elliott and I had to answer is answered, at least for us.

Potter Thompson has been a process of discovery. The process was brought about by sustained acts of aggression. We ganged up on each other. Since the concept had been mine, the initiative lay with me. We had discussed abstract principles, but nothing else would happen until there were some words.

I produced a draft, and the other two tore it up for me. I produced another. They tore it up. And so we went on, through draft after draft. I had to justify every move I made. Gordon Crosse would explain his problems in linguistic, not musical, terms; and Michael Elliott would point out each stupidity and *non sequitur*; and I would pick up the pieces and start again, criticised but not dictated to.

In this way I learnt our strengths and our weaknesses, and where to heed and where to reject. Finally, I knew when to tell the composer and the director to shut up; and they knew that I meant what I said. The next draft would be the libretto, good or bad.

Then it was Crosse's turn to endure. If we had worked well, my sense of language, which Crosse himself calls "symphonic", would give him enough music; and at least he knew that I could not interfere with his art. Yet I suspect that the director and the librettist were able to help the composer less than the composer and the director had helped the librettist. Music is a more private world than language.

The triumvirate was a good instrument. But *Potter Thompson*, which I am proud to have found and to have shaped, stands clearly as the work of Gordon Crosse.

9

Philately & the Postman

"Creative Natures and Communication" is the subject you gave me. By coincidence, last night I finished typing the novel I have been writing since December 1965. It is called *Red Shift*, is about fifty thousand words long, and the last twenty thousand words have come in the last twenty days. Therefore, I am not sure which is real, the book or this afternoon.*

In case any of us have met before, I apologise, since I have learned, from experience, that my participation in conferences does not work. It has become personally so distressing, a useless exercise for me, and, I suspect, for the audience, that I should not waste the time and the energy.

Before I made that decision, I was able to gauge that, within ten minutes of my beginning, abuse would start to flow towards me. The only people who ever just sat, and looked, and knew, and sometimes nodded when other people were behaving quite hysterically, were ladies in black. So I have been decoyed into thinking that I am fairly safe here.

I shall address myself to a theme, then it will be your turn to come back at me; and there will be no gain for us unless we are direct, since we are in a unique gathering at a unique moment. We have not been together before: we shall not be together again. So if I say anything that seems to be too dogmatic, I may be saying it in order to clarify the question in my own mind:

* This lecture was delivered to the Sisters of the Cross and the Passion, Mount Saint Joseph's Grammar School, Bolton, on 21 October 1972.

and you must be equally strong in your response.

It will not be the personal abuse I mentioned: the sickening, saddening kind. An example of that would be the time when a teacher of teachers accused me of having written in one of my books, Elidor, a vitriolic attack on the British working class. A German publisher, by the bye, turned down the same book because, he wrote, it contained a philosophy from which Germany had suffered too much already this century. Perhaps I ought to read the book again some time.

I shall talk about the demands of creative energy first. It is a dangerous thing to do, rather like performing my own appendectomy, and I shall not probe very deeply. I must be careful here with the word "creative", because I think that what it is for me is not necessarily what it is for you; and, from the failure to recognise the difference, comes a lot of the distress that teachers and I experience when we have to endure what appear to be our respective stupidities.

Now, from my point of view, the creator with a small "c", I work not because I want to, but because I cannot, beyond a certain stage, resist the internal pressure to write a book. I do not know what that pressure is. Some of it is connected with the period of my life between the ages of fourteen and nineteen; and that is a common element in creativity. Dylan Thomas said that everything in his work happened to him between seventeen and nineteen. And we should all remember that within us there is an adolescent who is still there, still remembering, still laughing, still crying. I speak only for myself when I say that the kind of activity I find worth the price, in writing, exists at the end of my ability to cope. There are people who work on a slacker rein, and those people I do not wish to know about. There is a man whom as a man I like, and whom as a writer I cannot evaluate since I have not read his books. But, as a writer, I consider him a blasphemer when he tells me that he will give only a calculated amount of time to a novel, and at the end of that time even though he can see the faults and how to put them right, he will not do so. That, to me, is an abuse of any ability he may possess.

Throughout our discussion I shall tend towards a religious imagery, mainly because I think it is apt for the subject, but also because we must try to communicate with each other, and communion is hard.

I had better say that I am not a Christian. I find that the quest is as valid a theological experience as the attainment. I should like, on my death bed, to be able to write, "I see", and to have just the energy left to put a full stop, not to whatever I may be in the cosmos, but to that part of it that can go no further.

In day-to-day terms it is not a problem. If I go through life accepting that there may be a black door with no handle and that I am going to pass through it to instant oblivion, then I must work twenty-seven hours a day, because the moment I have now may be the only moment I shall ever have. If, on the other hand, there is an infinite mind, there is an infinite spirit, an infinite power, an infinite wisdom, then, by definition, I am a part of it. I am a part of its experience, its manifestation, and it would be blasphemous of me not to work twenty-seven hours a day to fulfil that greater power, that greater talent, that greater energy. So I must continually put myself at risk; and if you see in my work things that are dangerous, they may well be there. Books are the most powerful means I know for the expression of truth and of lie, the most constructive, and the most destructive, product of the human mind.

That is what I see, roughly, to be the creative role as far as it relates to me. To go out every day and to risk everything. Anything less is wrong, anything less a denial. If you do not understand, I cannot explain it further; and, if I have said it properly, there is no need for me to say more. But we must make a clear definition and distinction here. I have spoken about creation, creativity, creativeness as a possibly pathological activity that may benefit others. As teachers, you may bring your own form of creativity into the classroom, but you must not ask a child to undergo that degree of exposure; you must not.

In the classroom, creation should go back to its root source, just as education should. The Latin "*educere*", to lead out, to draw out, should be applied, not to the adult's gratification or career: not in your terms, but in the terms of the human soul you should be enlightening but may be darkening.

Creativity in teaching is not to try to turn a random block of individuals into musicians, painters, authors, because any of them who are going to be these things will become them despite you, certainly not because of you. That creativity cannot be imposed. Let your creativity mean achieving the awareness in the child of the child's own potential, whatever that may be. Here you are the light that illumines. Show to the child, and those of you who are nuns can show it best, that there is no compromise. There must be no compromise, because, if there is, the best we can hope for is to stay where we are; and, if we stay where we are, we shall not survive.

My creativity is not always that of the classroom. The creativity of the classroom should be the creativity by the child of its own nature. That is: a coming into self-knowledge. I seek self-knowledge, too, but as an adult, alone (as far as I am aware). The child needs visible, tangible, assurance of support to take the step towards himself.

I can imagine what it is to teach where you have fifty children in a class. I know it is enough to destroy you. But it is your choice to teach, and, at the price of your destruction, you must not pull back from it, any more than I must pull back from facing the logic of the work I undertake.

Seven years is a long time. I do not want praise, but I do want you to know that three years ago it became extremely difficult to carry on, looking at the same blank paper, the same wall, waiting, a cat before a mouse hole, because, when that mouse comes out it will move quickly, and, if the cat is not ready, the waiting will have been useless; and this man-cat sat for seven years. I happen be a slow worker: others are faster. Whether they are better is immaterial.

Now I am faced with a hard question. Should my creativity be used by your creativity to elicit that other creativity of the child? At its crudest, should you use me as fodder? It is a matter of fodder. My anger with much of the teaching profession is that books are, too often, seen as no more than a medium for examination.

It really does seem that many teachers have never asked themselves why another human being should willingly try to make fifty thousand words cohere. The reason why I have stopped putting myself on public display is that I am not normally allowed to talk as freely as I am doing today. Normally I am interrupted, told that I am impertinent, which I may well be, and instructed what to write.

I am not criticising literary criticism. Tom Stoppard has recently dealt with this very well. He says that literary criticism (of plays, in his case) has nothing to do with the writer, the actor or the audience. Literary criticism is a perfectly valid activity for adults with academic interests, but it does not influence the work or the worker, nor should it. We do not expect a philatelist to be a postman. That is the distinction I would ask you to make.

Do not ask a child to be primarily someone who goes to a text to examine it and to explore it as a mechanism or a piece of language. Let the child get the more important aspect first: the emotion.

You know yourselves how that which is most necessary is beyond words. It is my job to use words to express that which is most necessary, to speak the ineffable, and I cannot do it directly. It can be only hinted at: it can be only hinted at elliptically, by using the words as a lift-off; that slow lift-off of the rocket, the first stage of which takes the energy, but is quickly abandoned, and the important part goes into orbit, and then into space, and so discoveries are made. Left alone, the child, in my experience, will climb into the astronaut's seat; but the teacher, too often, is yelling at him to come down and concentrate on the scrap iron.

I agree that a child's mind needs to be taught an analytic discipline. But are books to be destroyed on that altar along with the potential love of future reading?

My thesis may be summarised in many ways, but rather than repeat statements, I shall suggest a lead: art is essential because art is more real than the furniture of this room. You know it is true. Salesmen know it is true. Sell the sizzle, not the steak. The steak, once smelt, will need no proselytisation.

I am here only to show you what I try to be. If I ever succeed, I shall stop; which is why there is always a gap between the thing seen and the written word. What I can say is that last night I finished the best book, the best thing I have yet written. I have to define "good" first. "Good" is that gap made small; and what I saw I nearly achieved. The relentless self-criticism will come shortly.

There is another word I feel I can dare today.

As a result of writing this book, above all others, there are certain things I can relate to you and you can relate to your spiritual lives and your teaching. That is: I know something of what crucifixion is, because I know what Christ meant in part.

The words that He spoke have always puzzled me, and in the Greek the subtlety is marked. Usually the translation is given as "It is finished". The Greek word is *Tetelestai*. Implicit in the subtlety of the language is a sense, too, of "Now I can begin". "*Eloi, Eloi, lama sabacthani*" came first. "I'm drained. There's no more of me." Then, finally, after letting go of His resistence, "*Tetelestai*," "I've made it". He soared from the cross. "*Tetelestai*", "We have lift-off". And, because of last night, if you will forgive, and accept, me, "*Tetelestai*". I see the next book.

10

Porlock Prizes

When you asked me to speak today, you may have thought you were issuing an invitation; but you issued a challenge. This is the most difficult public statement I have had to make in my life.*

To think of "Awards and Award Winners" filled me with such conflict that my first reaction was to refuse, and it was only the vehemence of the reaction that made me have second, and subsequent, thoughts.

The first thing I noticed was that the vehemence was in conflict with itself. The argument was active on both sides of an opinion I had never consciously held. Until you asked, I had nothing to say; but, when you asked, the words came howling out. The emotional and non-rational response to the subject of today's seminar is: "Awards are an irrelevant impertinence, a distorting imposition on a book, and I want every one I can get."

I could see that this was not the most educated of responses, so I decided that I may best serve your time and patience today by dealing with the implications of my stupidity. Let me clear away the trivial and the uncouth first, so that there is no ill-feeling.

A writer has to live an insoluble paradox. He requires a public, and can achieve it only by becoming most private. I have been doing nothing else but write for twenty-three years, and have been published for almost nineteen. For four years no one knew

* This lecture was delivered to a meeting of the International Board on Books for Young People, on the theme of "Children's Book Awards and Award Winners", held in Birmingham on 29 March 1979.

that I was writing, and I had no evidence that I could learn to write. Now, if I were still unpublished, should I still be writing? Yes, I should. A more telling question is whether I should have written the books I have written, in the order I wrote them, and whether they would in all respects be the same books. That is: has recognition, of whatever kind, influenced the development of the work?

I feel that the books would have emerged as they are, but even more slowly. That is what I feel: and I know that I am wrong. The delusion of self-sufficiency is brought about by my concentration on the text at the time of writing it. Nothing and nobody can penetrate where this activity is generating its force. It is unstoppable, and knows only its own terms of reference.

Therefore, in the essential privacy, publication itself, never mind literary awards, is irrelevant. The only concern is to get to the end. Yet a book responds to one of the basic laws of physics: that every action has its equal and opposite reaction.

For myself, once a book is finished; that is, when I have discharged my responsibilities to the final proofs, I have no further interest in it. I do not read it. The printed object goes onto the shelf unopened. The total concern is answered by a total forgetting. I am not interested in what has been written, and find it hard to discuss my own work or to remember it. I do not disparage the work, but, by the time the book is launched and a response can be felt, that experience has gone from me and all my concentration is needed for the next. There is one egocentric divergence from this apparent disdain, and one fear. The fear, which keeps me from opening the book, is that I shall see either a compositor's error, or a gaucherie I ought to have caught at an earlier stage: or both. The egocentric moment is that I do open the book, but only far enough to see the international copyright symbol. Then, at last, I know that the book has been written, and I rejoice and emotionally collapse at the same time.

Such attitudes may be idiosyncratic, but they are proper. They are the effect of the demands of a privacy that is needed for any birth. An attempt to distract by dragging up the past obsession to the detriment of the present will elicit a snarl: "What book? What award? Who? Go away, you Porlock Person!"

At this level, which carries great emotional weight, a published book is a sloughed skin, inert and non-vital, the physical residue of an inner process that can never be shared. The book is a by-product, not an end in itself.

That is the triviality that makes me incline towards the uncouth. I forget that the sloughed skin may have a virtue that can come truly into being only once I have shed it.

The tendency to be affronted by literary awards relates to an inner stress, which is over by the time the book is published, and has been replaced by fresh crises. Praise or abuse cannot intrude. They have no bearing on the activity. But although this aspect is foremost in my experience of a book the book is, or should be, more than the symptom of a neurosis.

The book has its own life, is made by many people, and it is the life and the making that are helped by the award. Just as privacy is proper to the isolation of the writing, so formal recognition is proper to the achievement. My failure to differentiate between these two aspects caused the conflict that welled up when you invited me to speak. I had let the strands cross, and I was wrong. However, once the main issue is settled, a third and hybrid matter can be seen. It is true that I should still be writing if I had never been published, but I should be writing less well. I have no conscious wish to influence anybody through my work, but the environment created by a caring, critical readership is healthier than unheard self-indulgence would have been. Privacy needs to be inviolable, but the result of that privacy needs a response from outside, my objections notwithstanding.

The enduring creative act is between the work and the perceiver, and each re-creation says more about the work, and from each re-creation there builds a momentum, which grows to a collaborative response, which I become aware of and am helped by. The help is not so much a deed at a given time but an atmosphere. It is more subtle than applause. Applause tempts the performer to show off, to please, to repeat. All that is damaging. The help I mean is simple. It is the quiet nod, the unostentatious sign that what one does is worthwhile. This leads to an interesting concept. Literary awards, which are very public, are based on many private readings, each unique. The solitary reader, who may never speak about the experience, by the act of reading adds somehow to the communal response and brings about the environment in which the writer may flourish. Then the privacy of the writer and the isolation of the reader are transcended and become a reciprocal dialogue.

It is a long way from my petulant flurry that "awards are an irrelevant impertinence, a distorting imposition on a book, and I want every one I can get". I hope that I have disposed of "impertinence" and "imposition". But I can hardly escape the question of whether my ambition, too, is not here a little gaudy.

The subject of ambition is difficult for me, since the whole of my training and thought is against it, and my nature is to be aggressively competitive. One of the conscious factors in my becoming a writer was that I had been an athlete; and I had had enough of feeding on the failure of others. In a race, the runners had been there to form a pattern in my wake, and, although they did not appear to mind, I, eventually, did. I began to look for a way of living where the drive could be made positive, where the competitor to beat would be myself. Writing offered the challenge, and there is no doubt that it soaks up the adrenaline. I have found the race that cannot be won, and it needs no stimulus from outside.

My one irreconcilable worry about literary awards is that they may introduce a sense of competition into writing. If that should happen, then creativity is undermined. Literature would not be served by an award that claimed to apportion the absolute qualitative "best" to what should be an art. It would be a frame of reference turned towards conformity and against experiment: more aptly applied to the growing of giant leeks than to the writing of books.

I would argue the point strongly, outside my particular sensitivity in this area. It may not be possible to write a book so that every word is penned towards winning a prize, but it would be a disaster if such a book did win.

For myself, although I hope there has been some improvement over the last quarter of a century, I fear that my concentration would be divided if I were aware of a scale of measurement outside myself. I am still close to Charlie Brown in the belief that "winning isn't everything, but losing's nothing". That apart, a literary award can do great good. It may be only a token, in itself, but it is the visible recognition of that sense of service I was educated to respect. It is the antithesis of vainglory. It celebrates the work, and all who have made the work. It is not restricted to the holder of the pen. It is here, in the common endeavour, that my ambition lies.

I have dealt with the importance of a public recognition. Far more gratifying is the private. Unpublished, the books would be less than they are because they would not have been edited, and, for me, the relationship with an editor is the most rewarding part of my job.

The physical writing of a manuscript is so panic-ridden and relentless that it can be compared only to itself. There is no choice but to let it come. But the written manuscript does not live until it is read. The reading is the first evidence that the marks on the paper make any sense, because I have lost my objectivity, suspended judgment, in order to let the book come, and now I need help. It is the editor who rescues me. She (and I think it is significant that all the editors I have worked with, so far, are women) has to be simultaneously objective, ruthless, open, supportive and quick. No critic could be as savage as an editorial discussion, and few are ever as constructive. Without being partisan, the editor challenges me either to argue or to retract, but there is no acrimony. We are both at the service of the text, and we treat it as though we were discovering it together, which we are.

Then through the months leading up to publication, other people become engaged with us, and I see enthusiasm, an excitement that something new and significant is happening, and we are all equal sharers in the venture. It is a venture that, emotionally, never fails. The reason why it never fails is that I can rely on my editor to justify my faith in her. I trust her, and, as I have become more established, the trust becomes more and not less important to my self-confidence. And I trust her to reject my manuscript if it should ever be a poor one. With that assurance, I am able to let the story be what it is, not what I would restrict it to being; and this freedom makes for innovation and vitality.

I can never thank the professionals who back me up. They find the books to be their own reward. But, when "reward" becomes "award", then it is deserved recognition for skill and caring, and the contradictions of my initial vehemence at being asked to speak today are resolved and make sense. A literary award is the way a writer can celebrate the publisher, and I, for one, have much to celebrate.

Finally, I was asked to say what winning various awards has meant to me.

What I have said here has taken shape because you, by your invitation, forced the issue, and I have surprised myself by what I found I have to say. When I first received a literary award, although I had never discussed the possibility, my editor (as an editor should) knew my drift, and, at the end of her letter, in which she had told me the news, she added a handwritten line to the typed words of delight: "Don't you dare refuse it."

Well, I did not refuse. To have done so would have been to

trample on finer sensibilities than mine in order to make my own wrong point wrongly. I value the concern shown for what I do, and I thank you for obliging me to reappraise those values today.

I am left with one thought unspoken.

Excellence is always scarce, and, as the awards increase in number, I fear for the effects of diminishing returns. To those of you who are jurors, I would make a writer's plea. Never let standards slip.

The work must merit the award, if the award is to merit the work.

11

The Voice in the Shadow

Believe the fairy tales. What were fairy tales, they will come true.*

In very old, old times, one lovely spring, on a hot summer, a Polish friend of mine, Albin, was a part of an Arts students' tour of Eastern Europe during September 1939. He broke off the tour and rushed home to die for Poland, and nearly achieved his mission when he was surprised by a patrol of German infantry who were out in the forest looking for Poles to shoot. Fortunately Albin was bilingual and he had a fraction of a second to decide whether to die for Poland, or be a stranded holidaymaker trying to get back to defend the Fatherland. He chose the latter, and, as a result, in due course invaded Russia to besiege Stalingrad.

He was a part of a small contingent of artillery, and their method of advancing, and of finding food, was simple. They attacked any farm or cottage that they came across, killed the inhabitants and took the food. Albin volunteered to be the executioner. He would ride ahead, in his leather coat and steel helmet, on his motorcycle, machine-gun slung across his back, roar into the farmyard, loose off a few rounds into the air, throw his helmet and gun onto the ground, and shout, in Russian, "Don't shoot!" The genius of the plan lay in his getting rid of the helmet. He was no longer an icon of the Reich, but a teenager and a human being.

* Children's Literature New England: "Writing the World: Myth as Metaphor". This lecture was delivered at Trinity College Dublin, 13 July 1995. (An extended version of an address to the Story-telling Festival given at Battersea Arts Centre, London, 1 February 1985.)

He would then make social contact with the peasant or farmer, occasionally firing into the air, for the benefit of the approaching Germans, tell the Russians what was happening, that he had to have some food to show for his efforts, and that they must hide. He would then go to every one of the family and say: "My name is Albin. Look at my face. Remember it. I shall be back." Then he would empty his magazine, put on his helmet, and roar off back to the troop of artillery, a slaughterer of inferior beings and a member of the master race.

One Russian farmer made Albin strip while he killed and flayed a goat. He cut the hide into a continuous bandage, and wrapped it around Albin from his chest to his groin, then sewed him in. Albin wore that skin for two years without taking it off. If it had been discovered by the Germans, he would have been shot, because it was official truth that the German uniform was proof against all weathers. Albin says that, in the two winters he spent outside Stalingrad, it was all that saved his life.

Eventually, because the Germans were running out of ammunition, the order came to shoot at military targets only. Somehow, the Russian civilians got to hear, and there was an exodus. Albin was lying in a ditch beside the road, next to a fervent Nazi. A babushka came along, carrying her chattels, and, when she saw the men, she lifted her skirts and squatted above them. "I swear to you, Alan," Albin told me, "what she did would not have disgraced a horse." And the fervent Nazi groaned, and said, "We cannot win this war."

When Hitler announced that the army at Stalingrad would not retreat, but must die for the glory of the Reich, Albin turned around and set off to walk home. He walked across Southern Russia, and not one peasant or farmer betrayed him and some shared even the last of their food with him, because they remembered.

Soon after crossing the border he was met by the Gestapo, and he expected to be shot for desertion. But things were not going too well in North Africa, so before long Albin found himself retreating up Italy. By this time he was in command of a troop of gunners who shared his views about Nazis and warfare. He was on one side of a hill, and the Americans were on the other. The hill had been hollowed out to make a monastery, and, through the mediation of the abbot, Albin got word to the Americans that there was a group of Germans who wanted to surrender, and so a monk led out these bedraggled men to be made prisoners.

After a thorough debriefing, Albin was recruited into the American army, first as an interpreter, then as an identifier of members of the SS. Since every barrack room in the German army had its SS spy, this was not a difficult task. But, after several months at the occupation, Albin felt sickened and complained that he was acting as the SS themselves had behaved. The Americans asked him what he wanted to do. Albin said that all this had started because he had gone home to die for Poland. No problem, said the Americans. But you'll have to join the Free Polish Army, who are training in Scotland.

Albin took part in the D-Day landing and fought all the way into Germany until the end of the war. He was then told that he could go home. "But it is not now the Poland I would have died for," said Albin. So they asked him what he wanted to do. "Well," said Albin, "the only place where I've been happy since this started is Manchester, England." No problem, said the Poles. But you'll have to be discharged from the British army. So Albin joined the British army. And ever since he has lived in Manchester, painting, the holder of the Iron Cross, two Eastern Front Oak Wreaths, the American Africa medal, the Free Polish Army medal and the British Defence medal.

Now what can this have to do with mythology rather than black farce? The answer lies in the Russian winters. Albin was always in demand among his fellows, because of his drawing skills. At first he supplied the barracks with pin-ups. Then came the first winter, when the Germans were eating dogs, cats, rats and horses. Only one thing was required of Albin: explicit and detailed pornography. By the second winter, the Germans were reduced to boot leather and cannibalism. Yet Albin was still commanded to draw. He had to draw witches, trolls, tree-spirits, dwarfs, ogres, warlocks, goblins: all the creatures of folk-memory. The dying men were crying out for contact with the collective unconscious. They craved myth: the images of everlasting life. At the end, they wanted spiritual truth. What makes me think that this incident is of significance is that it is not the only time I have come across it.

When the British were deprived of their American Colonies, they were at a loss for a gulag in which to dump their political dissidents, especially the Irish, their petty thieves and social inadequates. Australia was a godsend, better even than America. It was as good as the other side of the moon.

The route from England was by Rio to the Cape and from there to Port Jackson, the future Sydney. The voyage took up to eight months, and all but a privileged few spent that time below decks, in irons and the dark. The shallow draught of the transport ships made seasickness almost perpetual. Though deaths were remarkably few, because the ship's surgeon was paid a *per capita* bonus for every prisoner that was unloaded alive, it takes little to imagine the conditions, both physical and mental, under which the convicts suffered. Yet they survived. They survived, not by plotting escape, mutiny, sedition, the making of future plans for villainy or the remembering of old triumphs, but by telling fairy tales to each other, which developed into competitions, and even into academic disputes and seminars, to establish a definitive text for a given story. And these convicts were largely illiterate. They had no written texts to compare, even if there had been light to read them by. The detritus of Britain became folklorists. Little may have changed since.

And, although bizarre, I don't think that it was his patent mental disturbance alone that led Rudolph Hess, during the Nuremberg trials, to ignore the court and to spend his time reading Grimms' Fairy Tales.

Now I do not want to get bogged down over nice distinctions between myth, legend, folk tale and fairy tale. That is a different topic, and we are all near enough in agreement about what we mean, for the purpose of what I am talking about. We are here to discuss writing the world through myth, and there is something to be said that may not be immediately apparent.

I should like to define "myth" as the dream-thinking of the people. Dream. And thinking. The difficulty for us, I would suggest, is that the Western mind first meets myth in its written form. When we learn the word "myth", in childhood, we tend also to link it to the word "Greek". Unless we become specialists, all our experience of myth is through the written word; that is: after the myth has entered history, linear time, been written down in linear words, thought of in lines. That is only the latest form of its development.

As most of the world still knows, the Western mind is a very small representative of homo sapiens. The majority of humanity is concerned with time in its entirety. In its purest form, because geography has made it possible, the Australian Aborigine has developed, over some forty-thousand years, the subtlest and the most sophisticated philosophy I have met. It is the product of an empirical pragmatism reacting with a lethally hostile environment. If it did not work, there would be no survivors. At its most extreme, we have the Australian Dreaming, where there are nine temporal dimensions, which we may barely comprehend intellectually, but which the individual, initiated to the degree, can enter and manipulate at will.

Once you are involved with the culture of dreaming, then you are also involved with time. And that results, among the Australians (and probably among others, but it is the Australians that I know) in considering learning to be a process of remembering. It was the same for the Ancient Greeks, who as usual had a word for it: "*anamnesis*".

Dreaming and thinking are uncomfortable bedfellows for our intellects, since our own experience of dreaming and myth is likely to be heavily defective because we are trapped in linear time. We know nothing about the real effects of myths, and we are not good at remembering dreams. Yet research tells us that most human beings dream each night, and lengthily. Westerners seem to have up to ten separate dreams a night, most of which they forget, or fail to bring into their consciousness on waking. That means that a considerable proportion of our total mental experience is undergone as dreaming and is largely devoid of waking logic. Australians who talk of the creative past as "The Dreaming", who consider that that-that-was-and-is-and-will-be is the real world, are not incapable of distinguishing dreams from waking experience, but they are aware of the former as equally essential to them as the latter. For them, dreaming and thinking are parts of one, unbroken spectrum. Such people, who are, importantly, preliterate, depend heavily on dreams for the formation of their myths; whereas more materially developed cultures, being less skilled in remembering dreams, will depend upon them less.

We pay a price for our literacy. Duncan Williamson, the greatest living storyteller in Britain, who has three thousand stories in his head, was illiterate until his middle age. Recently he said to me that it had become harder to learn new stories since he had been able to read. I also know an old lady, who is losing her sight and can no longer read, who told me that it was not all loss because she was finding it easier to remember the detail of what was important.

So seamless is the division among preliterate cultures, that they do not differentiate between dream, thought and myth. All are the repository of precept, wisdom, and what I have to call history, since we have no analogue for the word they use. Because the division is seamless, it is traditional to indicate to the audience that, in the telling of a special truth, we are entering a different time, a different space, an eternity that, by the telling, is perpetually being created here and now. The clock may still be ticking, but we, while listening to the story, are in sacred time. Hence the many "Once upon a time" formulae, with one of which I began today. They indicate by their ritualistic absurdities, their temporal and spatial word-play, not triviality but that eternity. All cultures have them, and Russian is particularly rich in this area.

"Long, long ago, when the earth had only just been made and the blue sky was being put over it, and it was all set about with wooden boards, in a place where met the longest rivers, there was once a man . . ."

"Ask; only it isn't every question that brings good. Once there lived an old woman in a house thatched with pancakes . . ."

"The roads are open to the wise, and they are not closed to the foolish, and once, or twice, there lived a man . . ."

"Once upon a time, when I was young and handsome, which was not so long ago, as you may see . . ."

"Once, long ago, in the golden holiness of a night, that never was, and never will come back . . ."

After the revelation of a truth in a dimension of timelessness, the hearers have to be returned safely to everyday living. Just as the start of the myth is delineated, so is the release from eternity, by a formal conclusion that is an act of play, no matter how serious the story has been.

"So Jack and his two brothers put the pot on the fire. And when the porridge is cooked, we'll go on with the tale. But, just for now, we'll let it simmer."

"They lived in friendship and in peace, they lived happily and they lived long, and, if they are not dead, they are alive now, and they feed the hens with stars."

"I once stayed in his palace, and there was much that I saw and much that I had to eat and drink, but it all ran down my beard, and not a drop got into my mouth and I rode home on a gingerbread horse."

"There are good people in the world, and some who are not so good; but he who listened to my tale is my own true friend. Now drink *kvass*, and go to bed. The morning is wiser than the evening."

"The owl flew and flew, perched on a tree, wagged her tail, rolled her eyes and flew off again. She flew and flew to the end of the world and the back of the sky. I've been clearing my throat to tell you a tale. The tale itself has not begun."

By reciting a myth, the storyteller remembers a creation, and, by remembering, is a part of that creating. It is best understood in that dreadful solecism "walkabout". In walking, the Australians speak the land. Their feet make it new, now, and in its beginning. And the land speaks them now, anew, and in their beginning, by step and breath that meet in its dance, so that land and people sing as one. It is a symbiosis of multiple time. They pity our ignorance in these matters. For the initiated Australians, the white Caucasian has, they say, "one sense less and one skin more."

In all societies, including our own, learning is a structured process. We do not try to teach a six-month-old child the Special Theory of Relativity. Similarly, in societies where dream and thought and myth are integral, there are versions of every myth for every level of initiation; and the final initiation is death. This means that a myth exists on a primary, secular level, which may be told to the whole community and to outsiders, and moves, by degrees, onto higher religious and philosophical planes, while remaining recognisably the first easy story, so that the individual, right up to the rank of shaman, is always aware of continuity and growth, of the simple coexistent with the complex and the esoteric. It is akin to learning, eventually, that "Jack and the Beanstalk" contains a Beatitude. How much simpler and more beautiful would Biblical criticism be if that were true for civilised, literate us.

Such a structured process is possible only so long as the form remains preliterate; that is, non-linear. Which means that the myths we have from history, and the myths that field-workers bring home, are the secular versions, even though scholarship may correctly detect, elements of the religious. But they are not survivals, they are pre-echoes. The people, however, in their varying degrees of initiation, or education, have the totality. In a few, rare cases, an outsider has been able to obtain, and to publish, a myth at both the exoteric and at an esoteric level.

An instance is Paul Radin, who collected the Trickster myth of the Winnebago Sioux in 1908 despite the warning contained in the esoteric version:

> This, too, remember. Never tell anyone about this rite. Keep it guarded secret. If you tell it, the world will come to an end. We shall all die. Into the bowels of our grandmother, Earth, we must send these words, so that by no possible chance can it ever come into daylight. So secret must this be kept. For ever must this be done.

Radin's expressed reason for publishing was that, if he had not, the material would have been lost, since he claimed to have gathered it from the last surviving shaman of the Winnebago. If he was writing honestly, then he exposed his unawareness of the relationship between the shamanic and Time.

It is my personal view that the material should not have been recorded. Only in linear time would it have been lost. The myth did not depend on Radin for its survival. Exposed to an unprepared world, his published text cannot be interpreted aright. It becomes offal and garbage: pabulum for such as the New Age mystics, who act as though knowledge does not have to be won but can be scavenged. It is a degradation of the myth as lowering as the demeaning of religion by the obtaining of a theological degree for cash. Ignorance is decked out as wisdom, and its adherents are led into darkness, as the myth warned.

The future holder of the story, of the myth, has to be conducted into the mystery in stages, to hear the truth from an adept. Every would-be Dante, who, in Dante's own words, wishes to "put into verse things difficult to think", must have his Vergil, or he is lost; and, even so, there is no avoiding the terror of the moment when Vergil steps aside, and Dante must go on, alone, with the image of Beatrice, in order to become Dante.

John Maruskin, in his essay, "Listening to the Printed Word", says it at its most haunting: "It is in the speech of carters and housewives, in the speech of blacksmiths and old women, that one discovers the magic that sings the claim of the voice in the shadow, or that chants the rhyme of the fish in the well."

Are we, then, lost: condemned to feed our imaginations with only the most secular level of myth, nailed to linearity? We are not. Can we write the world? We can; if we are willing to pay. The problem with learning to read and being subject to the writing, is that it ends up by being our only way into constructive dreaming. But certain people have innate skills, and they are the visionaries, the poets, those who use language that is the great constrictor when it is on the page. They release it into the subconscious by providing us, not with factual information of history, but with ambivalence and the paradox that enables us to interpret what is being said, and what we read, just as we would if we were dreaming. That is the way, via the poet, to the myth, to the truth.

The trap of the linear word and the thoughts that it produces is overcome for us by those people who can enter into the written language and extract from it this dream, this paradox, this ambiguity, which forces us to interpret. It is what I would call the "preliterate writing" that provokes response, and, in its provocation, awakes, differently, for every one of us, the dream.

For the Western mind myth is further removed from us by the failure of its providers to recognise the need for the material to be entrusted to the visionaries and the poets alone. The providers are, of course book publishers, and they do not know what they are handling.

Myth has been further diminished for us by its being out of copyright. With a few exceptions, this has resulted in the already weakened being reduced to a pap, because publishers have commissioned yet another gutless volume of "retellings".

Contrast this with traditional societies, where it is common for a storyteller to be forbidden to perform in public until an apprenticeship of twenty to twenty-five years has been served. Only then is it considered that the skill has been honed to the point where the individual may be trusted with the material and given the authority to improvise within it. And there has, throughout, been a master, both teaching and disciplining the novice. The master is all important, yet is unrecognised by the publisher today, and so the poetry is given to the unschooled, and the myth is degraded to garish drivel for infants.

That period of time, found so often, of twenty years or so, of the novitiate interests me personally. I write novels, but each novel has at its heart a myth, which should not be recognised by the reader, but provides the aetiology for the book. Yet I had been writing for twenty years before I felt confident enough to risk tackling the raw material openly. I am not the one to judge success or failure here, but it is significant that from infancy I absorbed, as if by osmosis, the precepts and music of the voices of masters.

Let me try to give you some of the flavour of the experience. If you know my books, you may hear the tonality of the voices of my masters speaking through me, but that will be a bonus, not a *sine qua non* of understanding.

I am a writer, and my duty is to the telling of tales through the medium of the written book, which will be read, either aloud to a group or silently by an individual. Although I must be able to hear and use the spoken word that I am interpreting, it is the printed text that is the vehicle. It may itself become again a spoken text, but I cannot, beyond a point, control or predict the voice that will speak it. That voice will most likely belong to a parent, a teacher, or an actor, all of whom usurp the position of storyteller without any questioning of their being qualified to do so.

The printed word, to be true to the primary voice, the voice in the shadow, must be proof against such performers. It must also communicate directly with the eye, and not obscure the story, so that it can speak to its other audience, the solitary reader.

An oral tale, merely transcribed, however accurately, will not fulfil these requirements. Some accommodation has to be made to phonetics in the transcript, and the result alienates both eye and ear; the words look, at best, amusing; at worst, baroque; grammar and syntax that represent plain speech become, in a mouth modulated to the dialect of white man's business English, an embarrassment, a condescension, an affront. Scholarship may be served, but the tale is not. The claim of the voice in the shadow is not sung, nor is there chanted the rhyme of the fish in the well.

In the written traditional story, it is not enough to repeat the words as they were said; the skill is not to record the moment of the telling, to act as a machine, but to re-create the effect of that moment for the reader.

The achievement of such a balance between the natural voice and the formal page is not easy; and it is made harder by the differing worlds that the two elements often represent; for, whereas the audience of the traditional tale is naturally in the community of a rural society, the audience of the book is to be found more among the sophisticated and the urban.

How to serve both tradition and audience in a book? Each writer has to answer the questions with whatever skills are at his or her disposal, and with whatever insight experience may bring.

My way is simply my way; another writer will have another; but one element comes close to being essential, if the stories are to be handed on as living entities. The storyteller should, as all apprentices are, be guided by a personal master. It is a craft to which a proper time has to be served.

My good fortune has been to have had four such masters who have thought it a matter of importance that I hear what they have to say; and now I want to let them speak, to give you an example of how the voice in the shadow may be heard. I shall draw on three of these masters only, because with them I share a commonality of place and of culture that I do not with the fourth. That fourth is Welsh, and the bond between us, though adamantine, is not so clearly visible as it is with the other three, and would, I feel, be a distraction here.

The place that is shared in common is East Cheshire: a country of lowland hills on the flanks of the bleaker Pennines; the land, and the language, of *Sir Gawain and the Green Knight* and the location of the Green Chapel. The culture is that of its rural working class.

The first master is Joshua Birtles. He was a pig-sticker and small farmer on Alderley Edge, where both our families have been long settled, though his must have come originally from Birtles itself, which is the next township to Alderley, while my family probably came down from the hills above Macclesfield, about the beginning of the sixteenth century, to cut stone in the quarries on the Edge. I abused Joshua as the character of Gowther Mossock in my first two novels, as a result of which I became aware of the questions his and my consanguinity posed.

Every Friday, Joshua used to deliver eggs and vegetables in his cart, pulled by his horse, Prince. Some of my earliest memories are of Joshua's britches, stockings and boots looming over me as I sat on the kitchen floor, and of hearing his voice, pitched to carry against gale and hill, jarring the windows. His hands were gigantic, spilling cauliflowers, cabbages and potatoes over the table, and themselves seemed to be producing the great bounty, without the need for soil.

He was huge in frame and spirit; he was almost not credible, so completely was he the image of a pre-industrial, bucolic ideal that never was or could be, except in the sentimental minds of the urban middle classes. And he knew how he looked. "You see," he said to me once, "I'm just at the end, like, of one period, some way."

It is an aspect common to all the masters I have known. They seem, but only seem, to be out of step with time. Yet it would be a mistake to think that, because a man is content to keep to the old ways, his mind is not up to date. It is not that such individuals are living in the past, but that their intensity of life includes both past and present; and from that security they grasp the future.

It was exemplified for me when Jos said, "You know how some people carry on if an old windmill has to come down: 'Oh! They're taking away a landmark!' Then, when these pylons go up, they create the dickens about that. Well, there's not a lot of difference between a pylon, in the distance, and a windmill. And, I mean, you can't hinder progress."

When I learned to walk, Friday became a high point of the week; for Joshua would let me ride next to him on the seat and to hold Prince's reins. And all this time, he was talking to me, and telling me things: the reason why a particular stone in a hedge bank was called the Bull Stang; that a hummock in a field above his farm was called Finlow because a king was buried there. When formally educated, I recognised that the hummock was a Bronze Age tumulus, four thousand years old. So, in every way, I came to know my place, and to see that myth was also memory.

Here are some of Joshua's words: the words he gave me as a child, and which I have kept safe.

"There's an old thing he used to tell me. If I was a bit upset, my father would say: 'Come here, lad, and I'll tell thee a tale.

> 'I'll tell thee a tale
> About a weasel and a snail,
> A monkey and a merry abbot:
> Seven good sons for winding.
> They rambled and they romped,
> And they come to a quickthorn hedge.
> E'en the millstones we're going to jump in!
> What must I do to save my shins?
> O'er Rinley-Minley common.
> Up starts a red hare
> With a good sort of a salmon feather in its tail.
> Having a good broadsword by my side,
> I shot at it.
> No matter o' that, but I missed it.
> Up comes Peter Pilkison
> Mowing oat cakes in the field of Robert Tellison.
> Hearing this news, he come;
> Tumbled o'er th' turfcote,
> O'er th' backerlash,
> O'er Winwick church steeple;
> Drowned in a bag of moonshine
> Behind Robert Chent's door,
> Chowbent.'

"Now what that means, I've no idea! He used to sing these little ditties to me. (He was no singer.) One was:

> 'I'll dye, I'll dye my petticoat red;
> For the lad I love I'll bake my bread;
> And then my daddy will wish that I were dead,
> Sweet Willy in the morning among the rush!

> Shurly, shurly, shoo-gang-rowl,
> Shoo-gang-lollymog-shoo-ga-gang-a-lo!
> Sweet Willy in the morning among the rush!'

"And what *that* means, I've no idea! Oh yes! Here's another little song:

> 'Oh, Taffy was born at Lincoln in Wales,
> Sold him again to darling-a-Noddy.
> He came over to England to tell his fine tales;
> He sang: Tither-o, tether-o, kither-o, kell-o,
> Kai nello!'

"Ay! And I think that's about the lot of those little ditties he used to sing me!"

When Jos was a boy, he used to blow the bellows for the organ at Birtles church, as his father had done before him. The time came for a new organ, and Jos was allowed to keep the old bellows handle, which he split to make the runners for a sledge to ride on the Riddings, a field across the lane from the farm, and so steep that it could be sledged all the year round.

"When I was a youth, we had this big sledge I was telling you about. It held seven people. And one Sunday we were sledging there; and Sam Read, that lived down at the farm here, he was younger than me, a young lad, and he'd been to Sunday school; and, instead of going in, changing, he thought he'd just have a ride down first: just have one.

"Anyway, he was the back man, and when we got to this ridge where the sledge did a jump and left the ground for about five yards, his behind slipped over the end of the sledge.

"He couldn't fall off, because someone had got hold of his legs (we held each other's legs fast) and he was dragged down, and all the gorse that grew there, and his pants were just about worn out, to say nothing of the gorse thorns he had to contend with.

"His mother played the dickens with him! So that was that. He never had another ride in his best clothes. But, at different times, we sprained two young women's ankles. Of course, it was such a big stop at the bottom, if you didn't put the brake on: get your heels out; and even if you did, you ended up a bit rough. Ay. But it was a wild ride. It fair took your breath away. It was a good one."

At the other side of the field called the Riddings, there was a brick cottage, divided into three dwellings. At one end there lived an old man; and, at the other end there was his barn; and in between lived Polly Norbury.

"Ay! Polly Norbury! She had the misfortune to lose a leg; and I think that embarrassed her a lot, because, after coming back from the First World War, although I went to school with her, I only saw her twice in all the time till she died, which was about four years ago. Only twice in forty years. No. She didn't seem to go out. No. I suppose it was a big shock, you know, to have a leg off, for one thing. And then living by yourself is no use. You just get tied up in yourself, don't you?

"I'll tell you a little story about that barn. The barn is eighteen inches higher up than the cottage floor where this Miss Norbury lived. Anyway; Percy Grainger and me must go kill him a pig one day, the chap as lived in the end cottage, and hang it in this barn.

"And I noticed that the water and, you know, water that was mixed with blood, bloody water, was getting away somewhere; just when we were finishing, I noticed this. It was going into her house. So I said to Percy, I said to Percy, 'I think we'd better, we'd better go now. We've finished.'

"This little fellow, he did get in a row, that owned the pig! It was going in there, because it was lower there, eighteen inches lower, her floor was; and, of course, the walls were old; and it had just had time to start getting through. I said to Percy, I said, 'I think it's time we went.'

"That's not why I hadn't seen Polly Norbury. No. I think it was having this leg off.

"Now, we noticed, both our children had slight accidents. One broke a collar bone; it was Ruth broke her collar bone: that was it. And she was only about two. Do you know, although she was a child that was full of vim and all that, it must have embarrassed her. It put a quietness on her. She hadn't as much to say for quite, oh, a few weeks, until it was better again. It has some effect. I suppose it's a bit of shock. Well, it's a bigger shock still, to have a leg off, like that."

Alderley had a mummers' play, which was performed annually, and jealously, by the members of the one same family: the Barbers.

"There was a fellow they used to call 'Serjeant' Barber. (He was some relation of Herbert's. He may have been one of the mummers; he was one of the Barbers, anyway.) Serjeant Barber. And he was courting a girl from Delamere; and it was in the days when they used to walk. And this Serjeant Barber lived up at Cuckoo's Nest, up near the Wizard there.

"Anyway, one Sunday he was there, spending the day; and it must have been about November time; and his fiancée lived down the wood about half a mile at Delamere; so she said, when he was going to walk home, she'd come up with him to the road. Some wag had put a turnip lantern on a post there; and she was frightened; and he had to go back with her.

"Well, her mother played the dickens when she got back:

'Come on!' she says. 'I'll go with you!' When she saw it, she was scared. He had to go back again that half mile, and then, eventually, walk home. And he just landed home next morning in time to change into his working togs and get off to work. But he said, on the way home, love left him.

"How far is it? Good Lord, I don't know! Twenty mile? It's from Delamere to the Wizard, anyhow! Ah! But love left him on the way home. And no wonder."

Fred Wright lived a mile and a half away from Jos Birtles, at the Beacon Lodge. He was a farmer, eight years older than Jos; stocky, with a white walrus moustache, and an impassive, Slavonic face. He was a man who spoke little. He had a reputation for surliness, but he was more shy than ill-tempered. However it was, the result was the same for me. I knew him from my childhood, but, unlike Jos, he did not speak much to me. Not directly. But he taught me the importance, and the communication, of silence. He showed, and did not tell in words, but through his eyes. At the end, what he did do was astonishing.

When Fred was in his late seventies, his wife, Sarah, died. The aloof man became more withdrawn, and people were worried for his health. But no one could speak to him of this concern. He was the remote patriarch, the stone-faced horse dealer, the alleged skin-flint. He was Fred Wright, and Fred Wright you could not talk to. But Jos Birtles did.

Jos told him that he was doing himself no good by going inwards. He should turn outwards. Fred said that it was not his way, and he was too old to change. So Jos urged him to write his memoirs: to get down on paper what he knew, so that, even if he could not mix with others, he would be communicating; he would be turning outwards.

Fred acted on Jos's urging. His writing, since he left school nearly seventy years earlier, had probably been limited to postcards from Blackpool and to what little was needed to keep his account-ing straight. But, because he had no experience, no sense of literary style or structure, he did not know the enormity of what he was undertaking; and so he wrote seventeen thousand coherent words without a sign of hesitation or struggle. He simply wrote as he spoke, letting the free thought and its associations direct the story. The impact is enormous, and a valuable social document. He inscribed it "The Life of Fred Wright and his Dear Wife."

"I was born in a house at Varden Town the rent was 1s 6d per week. I lived with my Grandmother we were very poor when I was 4 years old my grandmother sent me to the pub The Black Greyhound for 6d penny of whisky. It was pulled down in 1885 and rebuilt the same year but not as a pub. I had used to go on Saturday morning to Butcher Hattons for 1 shilling worth of beef and Mr Hatton used to put a slice of liver on for my grandmother and we had used to have a lb of butter 18 oz to the lb from R. Worthingtons at the Acton Farm.

"And then came the time to leave Varden Town and we went living at Daniel Hill with my Uncle Jim and then I went to Mottram school near to The Bull's Head. The teacher's name was Wilson, and he took to me like a father he used to shout to Fred Wright and say I want you to run me a little errand he would follow me out into the porch and give me a shilling to fetch him ½ gallon of beer from Hooley, and put it in the summer house of course ½ gallon was only 10d and the 2d left was for me also I had used to go and help Mrs. Wilson, with the washing, dollying all the napkins and I had used to take children in a three-wheel perambulator and I used to fetch her 2 quarts of stout 6d and hide them in the bottom of the dolly tub."

[At the end of childhood]: "Now I think that ends

another year. Anyway, I go back to Clockhouse with Jim Wright, that was 1896, me and Jim started to take two girls out for walks at night Annie and Edith Dunkerley from Manchester but my aunt went mad about that so we had to stop it anyway Jim left us and I drove the horses.

"Now we are got into 1897 the Queen Vic Diamond Jubilee it was a hectic year we had the largest bonfire that ever was built on Alderley Edge on Stormy Point. Now I have got another girl Amilia Leech very dark but deceitful took her to Blackpool at Wilmslow wakes paid for everything then she gave me the poke about three weeks after anyway she lives Brook Lane and has never been married now she is very fat and ugly, thank goodness nothing never happened I am positive I could not live with her. Now it is 1900 and I go and work for Mrs. Needham again at 12s 6d per week. I had the Irishman's rise, 1s less.

"Now we are at the end of the Boer War and we had a carnival every time we killed two Boers, now there seems to be girls everywhere we are going to a dance at the Public Hall, dancing from 7 till 11 for 6d. This was every Thursday night and sometimes Saturdays, but we had a long night once every month for which we paid 2s 6d but we had all the refreshments free ham and pork pies cakes jellies trifles Blanchmange as much as you could eat." [It is here, at the public hall, that Fred meets his future wife, Sarah, a farmer's daughter, and therefore far above his status, whom he writes of as "Ma".]

"One night who should come into the hall but Ma and I never seen her before there of course I had a dance or two with her but with her being a few years older you have not got the cheek to ask questions.

"Anyway, Thursday night comes again and Ma was there again anyway I said if you were going home and you have not got a partner I will walk up with you as we both had to go the same way home a few times I just left her on the road and just said goodnight and asked her if she would be there next Thursday all being well I shall come and it was the best day's work I had ever done because I was just beginning to be a wild card, going out every night nearly dancing and coming in at 2 and 3 o'clock in the morning.

"Now then me and Ma seem to understand I had got to going across the field to their house I had never given her a kiss not even tried till this night but it came off now we are courting proper now we keep on courting till the spring of 1904 and we got engaged. It was on the peesteps up Findlow lane then we got married on Boxing Day 1904 at Birtles Church. I walk to the church and I send a cab for Sarah from Len Smith's and Charlie Eveson drove them there anyway we went to the copper mines for our honeymoon."

[From the wedding, Fred Wright moves swiftly, by anecdotes, through the fifty-five years of marriage, as though he is being driven to record the death before he can go back and record the life. His description of Sarah's last illness, and of her death, is harrowing; and it is literature.]

"Hilda said she was a Martyr how she stuck. Then of course she comes home and is in bed, then in a few days Dr Edwards come in and reads the report from the Specialist now that knocked the stuffing out of me now she is a good patient she wont give you anymore trouble than she could help, anyway we bring her downstairs into the New Room. Dr Edwards said I must stop climbing the 12 stairs. Now she is lying in the new room and listening to the hundreds of people that have come into the yard, now she is very poorly for about one month only taking drops of water and Brandy and often unconscious. Then the last two weeks were the worst on the Monday she said am I getting better or worse

now these were you could not help her any and she always
had to Kleenex tissue always in her hand Now Hilda as been
stopping with her and then Ann came also but the final day
Sept 5 I was sat holding her hand about ½ past four in the
afternoon and she looked at me and said it will not be long
now and she rallied till ½ past six and she whispered 'come
with me' twice and I and Ann thought she had passed out so
I went out of the room while Ann was going to straighten
her up and she began breathing again and she rallied till ½
past ten but those last 4 hours did me more harm than all
the time she had been bad, I don't really know why she had
to suffer like this she was a very good living woman. I never
knew her tell a lie or sware and she always said a little prayer
at night.

"I think we were made for each other as we seem to be
identical in everything what I was thinking I am sure she
was but we have had a very happy life all through the fifty-
five years and the three courting years, I wish we could live
it all over again, one thing I wish she could have kept up this
summer and seen the sun and the gardens but no it must
not be but one thing I am sure I know she is gone to heaven
and I am hoping to meet her there, God bless her.

"Now I am writing tonight December 28 1959 as we went
to Edith's party we had only been courting a few weeks that
would be in 1903. I was driving the quarry horses I had to
give them the supper before we could go we started about
½ past 4 and got there about 6 for tea of course we had
to go on our bicycles and I know we started back about
2 o'clock on Sunday morning, of course there were no motors
or Busses on the road then now let me tell you after we got
married of course we were at Adder's Moss so one day she
said to me I don't think it is right for you to have to get all
the money to live she said I am going to let the two front

rooms which will bring in a little more money and she did
and she did very well out of it then in 1911 we left Adder's
Moss and went to Bradford House and she did the same there
letting the rooms in those days every shilling counted then
came a time when the ladies of Alderley Edge started to fetch
the poor children out of Manchester and of course Ma said
she would have some they paid 6s each with them that was
36 shillings per week of course that helped us along."

[The novelist in me would be thankful to be able to handle
pace, mood and time as deftly as that. But a novelist is making
a knowing artefact: Fred Wright is reporting his life.]

"Now I will tell you about the Boer War. It started in 1899
but there was no conscription like this has been like the
World War One and this second war. Now of course we had
fires while this war was going on. We had a carnival every
time we killed two Boers.

"I shall never forget one in Particular we were in the
Trafford, and 6 of us said we would have a cavalry parade in
front of the carnival and we borrowed horses and rode them
in front of the band. Now I will give you the names of the
riders Aaron Shuttleworth, Walter Read, Charlie Eveson,
Charlie Ford, Bill Gray, and myself now there is only Charlie
Eveson and me living out of them.

"Now we had all sorts of gun warfare 6 inch waterpipes
fixed to Handcarts. Of course a lot of fools were pulling
these. Now I will tell you about Krudger now he was the big
mouth, like Hitler was in the last war anyhow Burgess's lads,
Tom, Ernest and Jack they brought their old horse rake and
had a man sitting on acting as Krudger with a placard on his
back called himself Kruger King of South Africa now they
used to march through the village and go down Chorley
Hall lane to the recreation ground now Ted Lewis lived with
Sarah Henshaw who kept 2 cows and poultrey and old Ted

had found a nest of rotten eggs, and he told two girls about them and they got them and as Kruger went past riding on this rake didn't they pelt him with these rotten eggs oh I forgot I must tell you the names of these two girls one was Alice Russell and the other was Aggie Aston; Aggie is dead but I don't know about Alice and I think the war finished at the end of 1900 and that was when they would not have old Joe in the Trafford as he stunk the place out and he had to drink his beer in the yard and the Alderley Edge Temperance band* were all very fresh and they were playing in the road at the front of the Trafford some were leaned against the High School wall for to play and G. Cragg was sat on the floor he played the big drum they say he was the only one to keep time sitting down.

"Now then. Let me tell you about George Birtles who was a comical man now Over Alderley Chapel had just bought one acre of land from Lord Stanley as a burial ground so when the day of consecration were of course old George must have gone anyway he went home and said he should be buried there he said it was a grand place and you could see White Nancy from there and Ma Birtles said thee get on with dieing and we will show thee where thou will be buried and I think he is in Birtles churchyard.

"Now I seem to have forgotten about Ma talking about everybody else that is one thing I never shall forget she is in my mind night and day and I don't want to forget it is just twelve months she was just taken ill it was on the 19th. of February twelve months ago and she will have been dead 6 months on 3 March. What a pal I have lost which I am sure never can be replaced."

The life of Fred Wright and his dear wife. He wrote as he spoke. Yet

* Founded by Robert of the ophicleide, whose grandson, my grandfather, would be blowing the E flat cornet at this event.

I would ask you to notice that, even here, it is not enough for the written word to copy the spoken. No one wanting simply a story would read it, even punctuated to the received norm. The text is strong, all seventeen thousand words of it, because it is stark anthropology. It is not, in itself, the natural medium for telling a tale. But, for me, a writer from that culture, the language, rhythm, grammar, syntax and content are one and the same gold.

The greatest of the masters was Wilfred Lancaster. He was the miller of Swettenham, six miles from Alderley. The mill is a water mill, and the water is used to generate the electricity for the mill house as well as to grind corn and to run a saw bench. Wilfred's grandson is an engineer at the nearby Jodrell Bank radio telescope and built himself his own computer. It is the only water-driven database that I know of.

Wilfred Lancaster was always able to deflate me instantly. He cut across my intellectualisations with concrete logic. "Can you tell, Alan," he said once, after I had been plying him with questions about traditional beliefs, "which side of the church yew trees grown on?" I ransacked my brain for all that I had read about tree cults, the Tree of Life and the Tree of Death, and the merging with later tradition, but had to admit that I could see no significant pattern of ritual deployment about the churchyards in the cases I knew personally. "Why," said Wilfred, "they grow on the outside, dunner they?"

From such chastening experiences I learnt the lesson of the mythopoeic mind: use metaphor, never the abstraction.

The information I gained from Wilfred had to be got cannily: by waiting; by indirect reference; by elliptical conversation. I had to earn my right to move from the secular knowledge to the esoteric, and that would happen only when Wilfred judged that I was fit to hear him. So it was a surprise when he sent word that he wanted to see me. All my life, before, the only way to visit him was to drop by, as if through happenchance; and sometimes he would talk, and at others, not, allowing me to be present, but to watch, not speak. This time it was a summoning. I went.

Without preamble, Wilfred said, "I want to tell you everything I know. I've still got my wits, and I'm in good health, but it wunner always be so, and then it's too late, inner it? You see, there's things I can tell you that aren't in books and are on no maps, and it inner right as we should die and keep it all from other folks. It's nowt only right as we should let somebody else know, shouldner we? And it's nowt only right as we should let the young uns know, and then let it be carried on."

It was as simple as that. I would go to the mill, and Wilfred Lancaster talked, insisting on using my tape recorder, fluently, almost oracularly, without prompting or questioning, unselfconsciously and with force. History, legend, folktale, anecdote, gossip, ribald humour, tragedy, opinion and superstition: he never repeated himself. Here, the voice in the shadow speaks most clearly to me. You may find amusing some of the exoteric parts of the Divine Comedy through which I was led by my particular Vergil.

"It was easy enough when you got in the rhythm of it, Alan. You know, same as I say: you can be cross-cutting a piece of timber, two on you as know what cross-cutting is, and it isn't hard work; but get another beggar as dunner know what it is, and, same as I say, he'll maul your blooming belly out. And yet he thinks he's working! He is, by gum! And hard work for you, and all! 'I dunner mind you having a ride, but pick your feet up!', that's what I tell 'em. And they look at me like a cow at a cabbage. You know, when you tell them that, they wonder what the heck's up. But, oh, they'll blooming murder you, some on them will, for cross-cutting. Oh, no, bigod, they're murderous. But they dunner know they're doing it, you know; they're laying on, and they think it's cutting, but it inner cutting it at all. You know, your saw should cut itsel', if it's anything like. Oh, be beggared, ah!"

[Undertakers were frequent visitors to the mill, on the lookout for suitable timber. One of them gave Wilfred this story.]

"'So, anyroad,' he said. 'Did you hear of that job as we had,' he said, 'the other week?' He did say such-and-such a place. 'We were doing the job. They'd been in church; taken the corpse into church; come out again; put it at grave side; lowering it down; pulls planks from under; lowering it down by its handles; and the bottom dropped out! Man dropped out! Clatter! Straight in the bottom!' I said to him, I said, 'By the God,' I said, 'you dunner go to much trouble at screwing bottoms in!' 'Oh, no,' he says. 'They get these here staples and staple them in now.' Well, of course there was pandemonium. Folks was fainting, and all beggaring roads. They had to cover it up. This undertaker had to fetch another beggaring box and put him in. They had to take the beggar in church again and have another beggaring service. 'Ah,' he says, 'I got to know him particularly well.' Ah. The feller clattered out o' th' bottom. Ah! Oh ah! He fell out, right enough. He fell out!"

"Did you hear of Dr Jack as lived in Macclesfield? Well. Now then. He'd been to a Christmas party; and old Jack goes for bed; about two o'clock in the morning, a rattle on the blooming door. And anyroad, he gets up to the window. A fellow there. He says, 'Come on, doctor!' he says. 'I want you to go with me!' 'What's your trouble?' He says, 'I don't know'. 'Be down in a few minutes,' he said. Anyroad, he said, 'I want you to go up to Macclesfield Forest.' His wife, like, up at Macclesfield Forest. This and t'other." [Macclesfield Forest is a wild area of the Pennines, some five miles from Macclesfield, and fifteen hundred feet higher, up vicious gradients and over bad surfaces.] "He said, 'How much will it be?' 'Oh, at this time of night,' he said, 'ten shilling.' Anyroad, he gathered his traps up, the old Dr Jack did, and chap sits by him, like, in the motor, and away they goes.

"Got to the bottom somewhere, this Macclesfield Forest. About six or eight gates they opened, like. They sees farm, up at top; and he stopped at the last gate. He says, 'You'll do at that, doctor.' Doctor was out with his bag and for up. He says, 'How much did you say it was?' 'Oh,' says doctor, 'ten shilling,' he says, 'but,' he says, 'I haven't done the job yet.' 'No, but,' he says, t'other chap, 'you were half-a-crown cheaper than taxi man.'"

Sometimes the directness, the assumption of a shared background of understanding, can result in an allusive language that needs a commentary if it is to communicate. Here, Wilfred is telling a story to illustrate the truth of the belief that to order more wood for coffins than is needed for the number of corpses in hand, leads to the death of the undertaker, in this case within the week.

"It was this fellow, and he'd come for this; chap had died, like, and he'd nowt put him in, sort of thing, as fetched him and come for this here, a suit of coffin stuff, put him in, you see. And then he was wanting this coffin stuff, and it was that clean, you know, he'd stop a bit extra long and have another suit cut, you see. And then me uncle said, 'Ay, it'd pay a chap die to have a suit of that sort!' And that were it. Ah. But he had it in the week. Ah. Had it in the week, right enough. He picked his own out. He said, 'Well,' he said, 'I'll have that, and I'll have that, and I'll have that. And a bit of old shelving will do for the bottom.'"

Finally, Wilfred Lancaster on the problem of a man's having to be away from home, when he can't keep his eye on his wife's activities.

"It's a bugger of a job, then, inner it? When you come back, and they're singing, 'When you come back and there's nothing left for me.' It's there, you know! Oh yes! A slice off a cut loaf isner missed – unless you cut too deep. Of course, you've getten bread ready sliced now, dunner you? It gets missed a bit sooner then, dunner it, when it's ready sliced?"

It's by honouring such men that I know the Voice in the Shadow; by listening to the music of their cadences that I hear the Rhyme of the Fish in the Well. I take it into myself, and, with as much skill as I can muster and as humbly as I may, I shape it into my song. For them.

You might well think that a writer who ploughs such a narrow furrow is asking for oblivion, since he risks incomprehension on the part of his readers. But my experience is not that.

Somehow, and I think that it is a combination of a proper craft and of the universal power of myth, I appear to communicate. In one instance, *The Stone Book Quartet*, I thought that, since I was using my own family history and idiolect over a century, I had gone too far: that it was too personal. Yet, of all my books, that is the one that has drawn the most animated response from readers, of all cultures and races. They want me to tell them how it is that I knew that that is how their history was for them. And the book has been singled out for the Phoenix Award by the Children's Literature Association of America. Turning inwards, and going through the self, would seem to be the road to what, translated, the Australians call the "All-Self". How else could one square mile of Cheshire hillside speak to the world?

I would answer that, by employing such intensity, I have allowed that hill to speak its myth.

Here, to end, and to thank my masters, is a brief story retold by me, but not from them. I hope that it shows how I have tried to serve the Cheshire voice in the shadow. The story is called: "Johnny Whopstraw".

"I'll see if I can tell it as it was told to me; but I've got a bone in my leg, remember.

"Johnny Whopstraw was out walking one fine day when he spied a hare sitting under a bush on a common. He thought: What luck! Here's me; and I'll catch this hare, and I'll kill him with a whip, and then I'll sell him for half-a-crown. With that money, I can get a young sow, I reckon; and I'll feed her up on scraps, and she'll bring me twelve piglets.

"The piglets, when they're grown, they'll have twelve piglets each. And when they're grown, I'll slaughter the lot of them; and that'll bring me a barn-load of pork.

"I'll sell the pork, and I'll buy a little house for my mother to live in; and then I can get married myself.

"I'll marry a farmer's daughter; and she'll fetch the farm with her. We'll have two sons; and I'll work them hard and pay them little. They'll be that whacked, they'll oversleep in the morning, and I'll have to give them a shout to rouse them. 'Get up, you lazy beggars!' I'll say. 'The cows want milking!' But Johnny Whopstraw had fallen so in love with his big ideas that he really did shout, 'Get up, you lazy beggars! The cows want milking!'

"And that hare, it took fright at the row he was making, and it ran off across the common; and he never did catch it; and his money, pigs, house, farm, wife and children were lost, all because of that.

"And so the bridge bended. And so my tale's ended."

I first told that story at a conference of storytellers, and it was well received, especially when I revealed that I had collected it from Siberia. But my moment of smugness did not last. In the audience was Duncan of the Three Thousand Tales, on his first venture out of Scotland. He came up to me afterwards, his eyes twinkling, and said: "That's one of my stories, too."

It brought home to me that, though we may be the lantern bearers, we are not the lanterns. When Wilfred Lancaster summoned me and told me that he wanted me to know what he knew, I was put into a spiritual turmoil by the implications of his changing from teaser to teacher: of giving freely what he had hitherto kept close. I asked him: "Why me?"

His reply to the question may be translated as: "Because not many people round here now would know the value of what I have to say; but you do; and I trust you to handle the material and to be true to it and to me." His actual words were: "Because you're the only one of us left, Alan, with the arse hanging out of his britches." It was Wilfred's greatest compliment, and my proudest charge.

A story for you. A crock of butter for me.

12

The Phoenix Award Acceptance Speech

It gives me the greatest pleasure to accept this award: greater than you could possibly know. But first I must admit to a misdemeanour. You have not given the Phoenix Award to the complete text as it was written; so I shall try to make amends by reading you a portion of *The Stone Book*, transcribed from the original manuscript.*

I always date each day's writing, and put the time of the start. Therefore, we have, in the relevant section: 11 June 1975. 15.11. "Father came down from playing his music to mother. He sat at the table with Mary and sorted the stones she had picked with little Esther that day." And so on, until: "Father took a stone and broke it. He broke it cleanly down the middle. The inside was green and grey. He took one half and turned so that Mary <01.18. Thursday 12 June 1975> could not see how he rubbed it." The manuscript flows, with only one word corrected, for two pages, until: "'And I'm asking parsons, if it was Noah's flood, where was the urchin before? How long do <BY BED IN WARD 26. 02.35. 12 June 1975> stones take to grow? And how do urchins get in stones? <02.40. 50″> It's time and arithmetic I want to know. Time and arithmetic and sense.' <02.42. 40″>"

The next sentence is dated forty-five days later: Sunday, 27 July 1975. 19.49. "'That's what comes of reading,' said Old William. 'You're all povertiness and discontent.'"

* This lecture was delivered to The Children's Literature Association of America, at the University of North Carolina at Charlotte, on 7 June 1996.

There you have the complete text. It may not be literature, but it is a document which I treasure.

What had happened was that, as I was writing, Katharine, my thirteen-year-old daughter, had interrupted by calling out, "Can you come a bit quickly?"

My wife, Griselda, seven months pregnant, had haemorrhaged. The house where we live is remote. I remember flashes of what happened. I dialled for an ambulance, then for the doctor. The ambulance arrived, having travelled nine difficult miles, twenty minutes later. The doctor arrived at the same time. Griselda was rushed to the ambulance. The doctor stayed with me. He told me that my wife would probably survive, but he could say nothing for the child. There were three other children to be distributed safely before I could go to the hospital, fourteen miles away. The blanks in memory, and the utter calm I manifested, and the moderate speed and the care with which I drove to the hospital indicate shock. And what happened next must have been also an aspect of shock, but with strange results.

I found myself sitting in an ante-room to the labour ward. And I was holding both the manuscript of The Stone Book and a pen. The real world had been anaesthetised; but the world of Mary and Father and Old William was untouched. I looked at my watch, noted time and date, and continued smoothly with the sentence that had been invaded some five hours earlier. I was again interrupted, to go into the labour ward. And again I found myself sitting, this time by the bed and holding Griselda's hand and talking quietly, that world still in shock, while my other hand went on with its work, noting time and date, and, I saw later, logging the contraction times within the text. Then the birth, and its aftermath and concerns overcame even the ruthless hand.

I drove home in the early summer morning to find a house that looked as if it had been attended by the mad axe-man. Three days and nights of practicality and concern went by without sleep. After forty-eight hours, the baby, Elizabeth, was declared to be out of danger. I found myself sitting in a chair, with no crises, and no immediate problems. I realised that I had not been to bed for three nights, and rejoiced in an ambition achieved. I had conquered the need for sleep. Thirty-six hours later, I woke up, creased by the chair. And every reaction had set in, so that I could not write again for six weeks. But, before I passed out, something had happened in connection with The Stone Book that I have to recognise as an example of Jungian synchronicity.

The Stone Book itself had grown from a long-held need to celebrate the language and culture from which I came, and that had had no voice in literature since the fourteenth century and the writing of Sir Gawain and the Green Knight. The Green Chapel is ten miles away; and my father did not need explanations when I read the text to him in the tonalities of modern Cheshire dialect.

The characters of The Stone Book are my historical family. I have traced the Garner name on that one square mile of Cheshire hillside to a William Garner, who died in 1592; which is not bad for landless peasants who needed no documentation. And if a peasant family is in one place in England in 1592, it is safe to infer that they were there long before.

All through my childhood, every Sunday night was spent in the lamp glow of my grandfather's cottage, as his sons and their families paid their respects. No one takes notice of a child sitting under a table. And so randomly by osmosis, I absorbed the history and anecdote of a clan.

When the idea for The Stone Book struck, all I had to do was to tap, and rearrange, those memories. The holes I filled with a novelist's experience. So The Stone Book is historically correct, and, where history fails, the emotion is true.

After I left the hospital on the morning of Elizabeth's birth, the day staff came on duty. The nurse who was attending to Griselda asked whether she was Alan Garner's wife. Griselda sighed in resignation and owned up. The nurse then revealed herself to be my cousin Rita, whom I had not seen for thirty years. Rita went on to say that her daughter had always read, and reread, my books: not simply because of the ties. She actually liked them. As a result of this enthusiasm, the previous week her grandmother had given her a photograph of a family group, taken in 1890, that consisted of our joint ancestors, gathered around the seated patriarch, Robert, and his wife.

Rita asked whether I should like to see the photograph. Griselda, mere hours after the trauma of a premature birth, showed the reflexes of a writer's wife. She asked Rita, who lived next to the hospital, to go home and bring the photograph before I returned.

I arrived at the ward, no longer desensitised to reality, to find myself looking, for the first time, at Robert and Mary. I knew, intellectually, that it was a print from a glass plate that would have called for a thirty-second exposure without a blink from anyone in the group. But, emotionally, I saw the intense gaze of my people focused on me, demanding in silence, across almost a century, that I speak for them. They must not die.

Instantly, the whole of what is now *The Stone Book Quartet* precipitated, complete, a super-saturated solution, scarcely to change. I did not have to think, but to remember, and to use my skills in its shaping.

When it was finished, I thought that I had got it wrong. I had lost my writer's objectivity and had spoken in a voice that few would understand or find of any interest. It was too personal. Yet, of all that I have written, so far, *The Stone Book Quartet* has brought in the most deeply expressed responses, from all manner of people, in every part of the world. The question is always the same: how did you know it was like that for me? I can only wonder. Is the way to a universality best found by going straight through one's own being? It would seem so.

And that is not all. The unsought things have happened, that could not be foreseen, yet humble the writer, and make all the prices that have to be paid be as nothing when set against the gains. Of these, what I treasure most is that a teacher at an Inuit village school in Northern Canada used the books as a class reader with the children who were growing up between worlds. Their response led her to develop a project in which the children talked to their families, especially to the old, and gave new life to the traditions of their own dying culture. The children found a place that was theirs, and the old were restored to respect.

I took the battered photograph away, made a high-quality copy for Rita and kept the original. It was essential. If Elizabeth had gone full-term, Rita would have been on holiday when she was born, and there would have been no photograph to summon me. In my own post-traumatic state, I felt the command to get this, if nothing else, right. Yet I still had it to do. When it was finished, I asked my father to read the typescript. I had never done this before. I had always given him a copy of every book, but he gave me no reason to believe that he had read them, though his pleasure was obvious. This time, though, it was his displeasure that was to the fore. He read. And immediately he demanded to know why I had let the family skeletons out of the cupboard, and who had told me, in such detail, about them. It would have been impossible to have tried to explain. But my joy, in the sense of a purpose accomplished, was complete. The areas of my father's extreme irritation, I do not call it anger, were the parts that the novelist, not the historian, had written. A family of manual craftsmen had been served by a different craft of the hand. The earliest surviving example of writing by a Garner is that of another William: a scratched cross.

It is a tradition bordering on mandate, within the craft families, that each generation should do better, or at least other, than the one before. I was the failure. But, by granting this award, you have marked the journey from the signature of a cross to the symphony of a stone. And the travellers in between, and I, thank you for it.

13

Call a Spade a Spade

Knock him about the sconce with a dirty shovel: (Hamlet).

Act I: The Finder's Story.

In the summer of 1953, my last term at school, I was sitting in the Manchester Central Reference Library. I should have been annotating Wecklein's edition of Aeschylus' *Agamemnon*, but had become engrossed in Dr J. D. Sainter's *The Jottings of some Geological, Archaeological, Botanical, Ornithological and Zoological Rambles round Macclesfield*: (Macclesfield 1878). Page 47 had me hooked. It described the recent finding by miners of a number of grooved stone hammers, or mauls, in an old surface working, "from three to four yards in depth", near the copper mines at Alderley Edge, where I lived and had grown up.*

The hammers were quite distinctive. They were used as doorstops in the cottages and farms of the area, and I had found three myself on the Edge. (In later years, I learnt that identical artefacts are common where early metal-working has taken place. Those that I have handled, in Ohio and in Armenia, were all in a Chalcolithic context.) What was so interesting about Sainter's record was that among the hammers lay "an oak shovel that had been very roughly used". Sainter illustrated the shovel, back and front, opposite page 65, and to my excitement and bewilderment I knew that I had seen that "shovel", and seen it often. But couldn't remember where. I knew only that it was familiar.

Days later, in the way that such things happen, I was thinking

---

*This article, by Alan Garner, John Prag and Robert Houseley, was first published in *Current Archaeology* Number 137, March 1994. (For availability contact 9 Nassington Road, London NW3 2TX.)

about something else when I "saw" the "shovel" and where it was. I rushed to Alderley Edge Council School and cornered the headmistress, Miss Fletcher, who had taught both me and my father, and cried: "The shovel in Miss Bratt's room! Where is it?" Miss Fletcher, used to my manic ways, said: "I don't know, Alan. Let's go and look." We went to Miss Bratt's room, a nineteenth-century Gothic gaol, where I had been incarcerated in my second year of the Infants' Department at the age of six. Sainter's shovel had hung on the wall, immediately to the left of the door, next to a cupboard. The wall was blank, but the hook was still there.

"I remember there was something," said Miss Fletcher. "We'll ask Mr Ellam." We found the caretaker. "Oh, ay, there was summat of the kind, wasn't there?" said Billy Ellam. "But we had a big sort out when Twiggy retired, and most of it went on the tip." "You couldn't!" I yelped. "I'll tell you what," said Billy Ellam. "If it's not on the tip, it'll be under the stage in the hall."

I squeezed into the twelve-inch gap below the stage, lighting my way with Billy Ellam's torch. The space was filled with coconut matting, high-jump posts, Miss Bratt's fire-guard (we still use it at home as a towel rail), baskets, boxes, hoops, balls: all the clutter of a village school. I was lost to sight, and Miss Fletcher called anxiously after me, but I persevered, turning everything over systematically, in this exercise in educational speleology. Soon contact with the outside world was lost, as I worked my way into the dark. And, at the end of the understage crevice, the last object there, I found the "shovel", with the label identifying its provenance still (just) adhering. There was no room to turn around. I had to find my way back blind, pulling with my toes and pushing with my one free hand.

"Well!" said Miss Fletcher. "I think it's finders keepers. I've never seen anything like that performance in all my born puff!"

I took the shovel to the Manchester Museum, but did not get

past the desk. Despite my protestations, there was "no one available to comment".

So it began. I knew, from experience, my parents' habit of disposing of anything they didn't understand, or think of worth, and that compelled me never to leave the "shovel" at risk. It went with me all through the army, occupying the centre of my kit bag.

The British Museum declared it "possibly a Tudor winnowing-fan".

It was with me at Oxford. The Ashmolean was not interested and promoted it to a "child's toy spade: Victorian". The conditions of its finding were ignored. I stopped. There were other things to be done. So I kept the Tudor winnowing-fan and Victorian child's spade safe and bided my time. I knew instinctively and later intellectually, that the object was of considerable archaeological importance and trusted that one day I should find the sympathetic ear.

Eventually, the ear belonged to Dr John Prag. I baited the trap with some "Celtic" stone heads, for the recording of which he was responsible at Manchester. He came to see the two that I had. I showed him the shovel. The trap was sprung. And I shall never forget the sense of achievement as I formally put the shovel into his hands and care. The rest is prehistory.

I remain awed by three aspects of the matter: the tenuousness of the thread of survival; the unscholarly attitude of many archaeologists, who seem to work on the principle of, "If I don't comprehend it, it can be of no significance"; and the importance of the human ageing process.

I had not changed my story since I was eighteen years old. It seems a pity that we have had to wait forty years before I was sere enough to approach with any authority the university I had tried first. And I was fortunate in meeting the open mind of a John Prag. In my tetchy dotage I would urge all archaeologists not to dismiss the young. They do, at least, have better eyesight; and are capable of squirming through the lumber of a village school.

Act II: The Curator's Story.

JOHN PRAG, *The Manchester Museum*

1991.85. Wooden spade: the blade long and narrow with a steeply rounded end; one side of the blade missing, and an old split running with the grain between this break and the handle. The handle is short, and tapers to a point: possibly part of it split away, ? in antiquity. Probably oak. Max. total length 59.4 cm, length of blade 33.4 cm; max. length of handle 26.5 cm; max. extant width 12.3 cm. From excavations at Alderley Edge, 1875: presented by Alan Garner. Thought by Boyd Dawkins to be Bronze Age: dating confirmed May 1993 by accelerator radiocarbon dating OxA-4050 as 3470 + − 90 (uncalibrated) BP 1520 + − 90 BC, which, when calibrated, gives a range 1888-1677 cal BC.

(From the Manchester Museum Accessions Register)

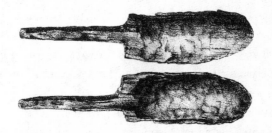

The date copper was first mined on Alderley Edge in Cheshire has long been a matter for speculation. Archaeologists (as opposed to mining historians) have generally leaned towards the Bronze Age: the date was first proposed, tentatively, by the Manchester geologist and prehistorian, Professor William Boyd Dawkins, who visited the site in 1874, when the Alderley Edge Mining Company Ltd. were carrying out clearance work prior to opening new adits at Brynlow on the south slope of the Edge, and who then carried out a further investigation of the site. The miners, like many local people before, and like Boyd Dawkins and his successors Darbishire, Roeder, Graves and many others, found great numbers of grooved sandstone hammers, and it was apparently simply on the basis of their crudeness that Boyd Dawkins suggested that the mines must be early, and therefore of the Bronze Age. Similar arguments have been put forward for other sites in Britain and elsewhere, where independent evidence has nearly always been lacking. The question was reconsidered in *Current Archaeology* 99 by Paul Craddock, who noted that at least two recent writers had cast serious doubt on the prehistoric date for Alderley and other sites, on the grounds of insufficient evidence (C. S. Briggs, PPS 49, 1983, and G. Warrington, "J. Chester Arch. Soc. 64, 1981"); Briggs went so far as to reject the Bronze Age C-14 date achieved for the Mount Gabriel mines (County Cork), on the grounds that it was from a single sample in a potentially confused context.

Neolithic flints have been found on Alderley Edge, but no securely Bronze Age artefacts. In 1991 a Middle Bronze Age palstave was found in a garden in the area known as the Hough below the north side of the Edge; at the same time Alan Garner rediscovered another palstave that had been found in 1936 at Common Carr Farm, on the plain a mile and a half to the northwest of the mines. Both find spots suggest these bronzes may have been deposited as offerings in springs or pools, and they need have no direct connection with the industrial activity above.

The mines themselves have been extensively worked in the post-medieval period, from the late seventeenth to the early twentieth centuries and, particularly in recent years, have attracted a great number of visitors and not a few vandals, so that the chances of finding evidence for early mining around the shafts are slim. Not surprising perhaps, that the Manchester Museum, as well as a large collection of stone hammers from Alderley Edge, possesses an object labelled rather confusedly as a "Stone Age iron pick" (in fact identified as Roman in 1905 by its finders, Roeder and Graves, and most probably from a nineteenth-century drill bit).

In 1979 a team from the Manchester Museum, funded by the Manpower Services Commission, carried out a new survey of the Edge, complementary to the cataloguing of the Museum's prehistoric collections, but the plan to section one of the "ancient" working hollows in order to retrieve samples for carbon-dating came to nothing for lack of funding and because of a change of direction by the MSC. In 1991 David Gale conducted exploratory excavations for Bradford University in two areas of the Edge, partly with a similar aim in view, but none of the organic material found was suitable as dating evidence.

There remains the mysterious shovel, found the year after Boyd Dawkins' excavations and dismissed by Warrington as "of no significance for independent dating". Indeed, he pointed out that wooden shovels were in use in the ore treatment works at Alderley at the time of its discovery.

> As some miners were at work on the Edge, they came upon a large collection of stone implements, consisting of celts or adzes, hammerheads or axes, mauls, etc. from one to two feet below the surface . . . and others were left in some old diggings of the copper ore, from three to four yards in depth, along with an oak shovel that had been very roughly used.

So Dr Sainter in 1878, repeated by Roeder in the *Transactions of the Lancashire and Cheshire Antiquarian Society* for 1901; and (with the last illustration I have seen of the shovel) by William Shone in *Prehistoric Man in Cheshire* (1911). Since then it had vanished. It seemed to have become another of the legends of Alderley Edge. "If only I could find out what had happened to that shovel," remarked David Gale, in wistful ignorance, as we rattled in an elderly train out to his first meeting with Alan Garner.

There are few moments in any museum curator's life when he does not really believe he is seeing what is laid before him. One's colleagues, more senescent, more cynical or just less gullible, tended not to believe it. Not, perhaps, a Tudor winnowing-fan, but very probably a peat-cutter's spade, no older than medieval, they said. No one argued with the circumstances of the discovery, but the fact remained that the dating of evidence for that context, the stone hammers, were themselves not properly dated. The donor bravely agreed to our seeking a radiocarbon date for the shovel, and with the collaboration of Velson Horie, Keeper of Conservation at the Manchester Museum, we submitted an application to the Radiocarbon Accelerator Unit at the Research Laboratory in Oxford.

The rest is science. Although such shovels have been found in other "primitive" mining contexts, what is exciting for the archaeologist is not only that this one (an object of great interest in its own right because of its exceptional condition and unusual history) thus belongs to the Middle Bronze Age, but also that activity in the mines themselves can now be firmly dated at least to the Middle Bronze Age, and probably to the early part of that period. To judge by the great quantities and variety of the stone hammers that have been found, that Bronze Age activity must have been considerable.

Legends have a way of leading to the truth.

*   *   *

Act III: The Scientist's Story.
RUPERT HOUSELEY, *Oxford Research Laboratory for Archaeology*

In September 1992 John Prag and Velson Horie approached me about the possibility of getting a radiocarbon date on a wooden shovel which had been donated to the Manchester Museum. On hearing about the Alderley Edge spade the thought crossed my mind "wooden objects seem to be in fashion" since only a few months before, I and my colleagues at the Oxford Radiocarbon

Accelerator Unit had been involved in dating a series of wooden objects: a wheel, longbow, a yoke and some bowls, from the collections of the National Museums of Scotland. When John Prag sent me a photograph of the object, I was struck by how similar it was to the peat-diggers' spades I had seen in old pictures from the Somerset Levels. As to its age, who (or what) could tell?

The answer was to "what" rather than "who", and it lay in the wood from which the shovel had been made. As all users of radiocarbon dating will know, the possibility comes from the fact that a living tree takes up 14C from the atmosphere and incorporates it into its growth rings. The atoms of 14C decay with time and from this we tell the age. By determining the date of the wood one arrives at an approximate value for the time of manufacture of the shovel, although, strictly speaking, the wood could have been worked into the form of a shovel any time afterwards.

Late in 1992, once we had heard that the dating would be supported under the programme funded by the Science and Engineering Research Council, the next set of things to do was to think about how much wood to take, from where it would be taken, and to decide whether there was any sign of past treatment by preservatives.

As Alan Garner has shown, although the "recent" history of the shovel was known, or could in part be inferred, what the original Victorian miners may have done to the shovel was not known, and so we had to assume a "preservative" may have been applied to prevent its disintegrating. It was partly to minimise potential problems from this that Velson Horie drilled into the shovel, discarding the outer discoloured surface, to collect one hundred milligrams. (¹⁄₁₀ of a gram) of clean "saw-dust". This proved more than enough for a date.

A reflux wash with organic solvents was added to cope with any residual amounts of potential preservative. This rounded off the process: the result is chemistry and physics.

The resultant date 3470 + − 90 BP (OxA-4050) puts the age of the wood firmly in the first half of the second millennium BC, the shovel into the Middle Bronze Age, and, by implication, the mining of copper back into the prehistoric past. All because of a chain of some rather improbable events.

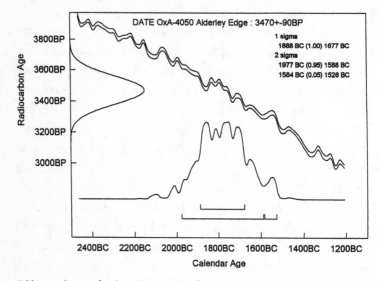

Calibration diagram for the radiocarbon date for the wooden shovel. The radiocarbon date of 3470 Before Present (left of diagram) calibrates to a date centring on 1750 BC (time below the diagram)

14

The Beauty Things

High in the skies above Belorus, a man was plunging to earth. He saw another man soaring up towards him at the same speed. As they passed each other, the man who was rising shouted, "Good morning, Comrade! What is your job?"

"Good morning to you, Comrade!" said the man who was falling. "I design parachutes. And what job is yours?"

"I am a bomb disposal expert," said the other.*

That story was told to me by a Russian Professor of Folklore in Moscow in 1986. His special area of research was the xenophobic joke, and he said that every country in Europe had an area that was, by tradition, populated by the inept and/or irrational: a Place of Fools. He told me that, historically, every Slav considered the Slav to the west of him to be inferior, and he had developed a thesis, which I would not like to have to subject to rigorous scrutiny, that the Place of Fools always lay to the west.

"And that," he said, "is why the English have Irish Jokes." He went on to explain that the cause of there being a Place of Fools was xenophobia, in its original exact meaning of "fear of the stranger", rather than in its more modern use as "dislike of the stranger".

It was an interesting conversation, but I did not have the knowledge to test it for flaws. However, it did set me thinking about the relationship between Wales and its marcher counties,

* This lecture was delivered to The Conference of the Welsh Academy, on the theme of "The Influence of *The Mabinogion* on Contemporary Authors" at Abergavenny on 8 November 1996.

especially my native Cheshire. I realised that, although I had been brought up to have strong opinions about the Welsh, I knew of no Welsh Jokes. The antipathy was more the paranoia of neighbours than a xenophobia. One example will show the difference. My mother drilled into me from earliest childhood that the Welsh were not to be trusted, nor was I ever to have anything to do with a Welsh girl, because "their eyes are too close together". That was a serious warning, not a joke.

I plundered my mind for a Welsh Joke, yet could find none. The nearest I came was in an anecdote about Welshness, told by the late Lord Elwyn Jones, so there can be no charge of racism laid against the story. It is, no doubt, apocryphal, but no less true for that.

Lord Elwyn was driving his car across mid-Wales. He was high in the mountains, in cloud, and thoroughly lost. He saw a small, old man, cap on head, sack on shoulders. He stopped the car, and said, "Excuse me. Can you tell me where I am?" The old man looked him slowly up and down, down and up, and replied, "You are in a car."

Elwyn Jones said, afterwards, that here was the perfect answer to a Parliamentary Question. It is concise. It is accurate. It tells you nothing that you want to know.

More to my point, it certainly was not Irish, in the English, idiomatic, pejorative use of the word. It reminded me more of my father, who was a quiet, gently spoken, kind man, of little formal education and few words. He was a painter and decorator, and I remembered being with him one day as he was up a ladder, painting a house on an isolated road. An open-topped sports car pulled up. In it were two parodies of the chinless wonder English middle class, each wearing his stitched-peak brown cap. The driver started badly with, "I say, my man!" My father rested his brush. "Which is the way to Prestbury?"

"What end do you want?" said my father.

"What end?" said the driver. "Prestbury!"

"Oh, come on," said the passenger. "The man's a fool." With the timing of a professional, in the silence before the exhaust roared, my father said, "I may be a fool. But I'm not lost."

The old Welshman and my father could have spoken each other's lines. But my father was not Welsh. Was he?

I thought further. Yes. Without "The Troubles", we were queasy about the Irish, in an amorphous way. And there was antagonism, but not fear, with regard to the Welsh. But, cry you mercy, we did not have to go to Wales to find antagonism. My own village was perpetually at war with the next one, two miles away: so much so, that the natives never refer to the places by their map names of "Alderley" and "Wilmslow", but as Sodom and Gomorrah. And to go to the hilltop settlement of Mow Cop was to risk grievous bodily harm. On Mow Cop, in my parents' youth, the natural reaction to a stranger was to beat him up on sight and to wrap his bicycle around his neck.

I have met only one instance of genuine Anglo-Welsh antagonism, and here both sides were provocative. My secondary education uncovered in me a linguistic ability above the norm. I appeared to soak up languages without effort, and I became a Classicist. In my last year at school, we went for a day trip to Tomen-y-Mur. The weather was hot. Before setting off back to Manchester in the coach, we stopped at Pentrefoelas for sustenance. There were about twelve of us, and our form master.

As we entered the shop, we interrupted an animated conversation that was being conducted in English, but, at the moment the Saxons appeared, everybody switched to Welsh. It was all a bit pointed. We stood there, feeling foolish; then our form master turned to us and asked us, in Greek, what we wanted to buy. So, possibly for the first time in Wales, a shopping list was drawn up in Attic Greek, and total silence from the other customers. Then, insult to injury, the list completed, our form master conveyed the requirements to the shopkeeper in fluent Welsh. It is a matter of record that we, and the coach, left Pentrefoelas unscathed.

However, all the way home, my head was filled with those few seconds of music I had heard in the shop. And, when I got home, I annoyed my parents by using every spare moment I could to find a wavelength on the ancient radio that, through the crackling, would let me hear Welsh. It was a change from Geraldo and from Forces' Favourites that was not appreciated.

I felt that I understood this language without knowing what it was saying. I could not learn, for lack of facilities, but the sensation was one more of remembering. It was as if I were hearing the knights, who lay in the cave with their king under the hill behind our house, talking in their sleep.

When, three years later, I began to write my first book, which is about that hill and those knights, I knew that the personal names of my other-worldly characters could not be synthetic and had to pre-date the English. So I came upon Skene's *Four Ancient Books of Wales*, and on something called *The Mabinogion*. And I was angry.

Why had I been filled with so many alien tongues and made especially proficient in Latin and Greek, whose sounds were wondrous, but whose tales were, for me, then, as bloodless and as cold as their marble? Why had I been kept from a language that not only sounded to be "mine", but also told its stories as I dreamed my dreams? I read that the material was obscure. But, even in translation, it was not obscure to me. Why should something be called "obscure" because it spoke fact as poetry, history as legend, sound as sense? The boon list in "Culhwch ac Olwen" changed me for ever in my heart. When I read *Preiddeu Annwfn* (*The Spoils of the Otherworld*), the hairs of my neck rose, as they do to this day.

> Complete was the grave of Gwair in Caer Sidi,
> In the tale of Pwyll and Pryderi.
> No one before him went into it.
> A heavy blue chain held the faithful youth,

And before the Spoils of Annwfn gloriously he sings,
And for ever the song shall last.
Three times the fullness of Prydwen we went into it.
Except seven, none came from Caer Sidi.

Am I not worth the fame to be heard in song?
In Caer Pedryvan, four times turning;
The first word from the cauldron, when was it spoken?
Is it not the cauldron of the Chieftain of Annwfn?
What does it mean to do?
It will not boil the food of a coward.
A flashing bright sword to him was raised
And left in the hand of Lleminawg.
And before the gate of the Cold Place
The horns of light shall be burning.
And when we went with Arthur in his splendid labour,
Except seven, none came back from Caer Vedwyd.

Am I not worth the fame to be heard in song?
In the four-cornered castle, in the island of the strong door,
Where twilight and the black night move together
Bright wine was the offer of the host.
Three times the fulness of Prydwen we went on sea.
Except seven, none came out of Caer Rigor.

I will not let praise to the lords of letters.
Beyond Caer Wydyr they saw not the might of Arthur.
Sixty hundred men stood on the wall.
It was hard to speak to their sentinel.
Three shiploads of Prydwen there went with Arthur,
Except seven, none came from Caer Golud.

I shall not give place to those with trailing shields.
They know not on what day that Chieftain arose.
They know not on what day, or what was the cause of it,

> Or on what hour of the splendid day that Cwy was born,
> Who caused that he should not go to the Dales of Devwy.
> They know not the brindled ox, thick his head-band.
> Seven score knobs in his collar.
> And when we went with Arthur of anxious memory,
> Except seven, none came out of Caer Vandwy. . .

Here was a multi-level logic that gave me no problem. Here was a language that spoke straight. How could some Welsh scholars complain, for instance, of The Third Branch of *The Mabinogion*, that it is "a medley of themes that are hard to disentangle", or that to compose *The Mabinogion* could be likened to trying to create art from a demolition site? The answer was obvious, to me. In order to understand *The Mabinogion*, especially "The Four Branches", and "Culhwch ac Olwen", it was necessary to have the ear of a poet as well as the intellect of a scholar, and to realise that this tongue called Welsh held sound to be as important as sense.

The Mabinogion, at first glance, is a rag-bag of Celtic genius, made of fragments of tales that have cohered as, through the millennia, they have rolled across lands and languages from their Indo-European source, to end up as a tangle of seeming flotsam and jetsam of story upon the Atlantic coast. Though unmistakably Celtic in form and content, which explains the repetitive onomastic elements in the stories, which the Celt uses as tent pegs to pin them down firmly and finally, against being blown out to sea, time and time again, elements of the *Mahabharata* and the *Rig Veda* show through.

The result is a masterpiece, mesmeric in its cultural imagination, its gods euhemerised, yet, since it is composed of archetype and metaphor, it is universal and timeless. Where some may see the rubble of a demolition site, I see the perfection of a beaver's dam: heterogeneous in detail, yet whole.

So I wrote my first book, *The Weirdstone of Brisingamen*, prefacing it with the Legend of Alderley, the myth of the Sleeping Hero, as taught to me by my grandfather, who knew, though he could not have put it into these words, that it was our inheritance and truth.

As a result, something extraordinary happened. The following letter arrived from Professor Thomas Jones in Aberystwyth.

> Dear Mr Alan Garner,
>
> About eighteen months ago, I was editing a sixteenth-century Welsh version of the Arthurian Cave legend for publication in a volume to be presented to Professor M——— S——— of Warsaw. The nearest parallel known to me was the Alderley legend about Merlin, and a colleague of mine drew my attention to it in *The Weirdstone of Brisingamen*. Previously, I had relied on the version communicated to me by E. Vinaver. May I say that the version you give is the purest that I have come across anywhere.

What a circle of perfection. I was able to write back to Professor Jones and to tell him that, without his and Professor Gwyn Jones' collaborative translation of *The Mabinogion*, he would not have found this "purest version", taught by a Cheshire smith to his grandson, where neither the Sleeper nor the Guardian is named before the literary impositions of the Romantics of the nineteenth century.

Then I wrote to Professor Gwyn Jones. He did not reply immediately.

> July 11 1976
>
> Dear Alan Garner,
>
> Pray read on, though you might be forgiven for throwing a letter from me on to the fire, dunghill, or rubbish collector's cart. Even assuming that it reaches you.
>
> You wrote to me on September 24, 1965, a most courteous and generous letter. At the same time, you asked for my opinion of the form or meaning of a few names in "The Fourth Branch of Mabinogi". I won't attempt explanations: I have none; or offer excuses; none are possible. But you

surely received no reply from me. I retired three years ago, and College has very kindly given me the use of a room, which helps with my book problem, and carries with it the inestimable bonus of a parking lot. The Arts Faculty was then about to move into a new building; so, for a year, I had a room on the top floor of the rightly-named Tower Block, from which, on sunny days, I could see Patagonia. But now I have a snug badger's lair, either till I tire of it or the terriers bite my tail off.

The relevance of this to me is that I have twice shifted my books and papers wholesale, and to you that your letter of 1965 fell on to the floor as I did some determined sorting last week. I have no recollection of having seen it before, and must wonder whether I set it aside at home or in College as I read your admirable *Elidor*. And yet your Blodeu(w)edd query sounded a note. Perhaps I passed it on to my friend and partner Thomas Jones (who died, I am sorry to tell you, in 1972). It is certain that, if I did, he replied to you, for he was too courteous and generous in measure with his immense learning. But all such fault as there is, is mine.

If I were sure of finding you at your 1965 address, I would be sending you a book as a token of my esteem. Please let me know if my letter finds you safely, and then, if you will bury the hatchet as deeply as I buried your letter, the book shall follow. And that will give me great pleasure.

I send my good wishes and my congratulations on your books. Oh, and *The Mabinogion* has received further attention for its new edition of 1974 (it appeared in 1975), and that too I should like you to accept at my hand.

[Apropos *The Owl Service*], my friend Brenda Chamberlain had a lovely sheepdog named Gwyn. He was of the female kind. As Fats Waller used to say: "One never knows, does one?"

* * *

He sent both books. *The Mabinogion* I value for its inscription; the other, because it is so badly edited, so overwhelmed by compositor's errors, that Gwyn Jones turned it into its own critical text by larding it with such actionable invective, marginalia and footnotes, that it is a unique and colourful treasure.

I met Gwyn Jones at Aberystwyth some years later, where he sat in on what I thought was a pedantic and uninspiring lecture that I gave on linguistics. But immediately afterwards he came up to me and said, "You're just an old Welsh mystic."

We were taken out to dinner. We were served lasagne. Some way into the meal, the host asked would anyone like to drink wine. There was a Jones/Garner chorus of "Yes!" The six of us shared one bottle of sweet, warm white wine.

Gwyn Jones and I sipped. Our eyes met. And he quoted from the *Gododdin*.

"Their lives was the price for their feast of mead." The Great Man was declaiming Great Poetry. Silence fell. All he said next was, "But I don't think that I shall be volunteering for Catterick tonight."

[The *Gododdin* is the earliest Scottish/Welsh poem, of about 600 AD, which describes the willing suicidal attack on Catterick by mercenaries who had spent the previous year in Edinburgh drinking alcohol as their payment. Only one is said to have survived: Aneirin, the writer of the poem.]

The years between the two Jones letters had been taken up by my reworking, which is necessary if a story is to continue to live, or my pillaging, if you do not agree, of *The Mabinogion* and most other Celtic texts.

The glaring example, which was deliberate, is *The Owl Service*. But, and let it remain the field of scholars, there is not a single book I have written that is not as solidly derived from Celtic material, though less obviously so. To begin to list examples would be pointless and tedious: tedious, for its length, and pointless, since you will know that there is scarcely an element in Celtic stories, including *The Mabinogion*, that is not found elsewhere, in one guise or another throughout Europe and Asia. That is not what I mean when I speak of derivation from Celtic material.

What I owe to the Celtic mind is the realisation that language is music, and it is that which I must write. It is so completely a part of my psyche, that the theme of this conference, "The Influence of *The Mabinogion* on Contemporary Authors" could be answered by this author simply as, "Total", and we could all have an early night.

Yet there is something more to be said.

Because of what I have described, for me, *The Mabinogion* is less a text than a state of mind or being. Despite the onomastic tent-pegs, *The Mabinogion*, though it may not fall into the sea, does not stay fixed. It is, as one example, all around me where I live in East Cheshire.

Late this summer, as I began the research for my next book, I came across a reference to a field twelve miles from my house which was called, in 1841, Osbaldestone Croft. I went. There, against the drystone wall, was a menhir, previously unrecorded. The name is pure Old English, and means "the stone of the shining god". But I think it is a translation. Of what? Four miles away is the Green Chapel of Sir Gawain, a dramatic natural fissure in the rock. Its name, throughout recorded time, has been Ludchurch. Osbaldestone led me up into a hanging valley, called Thursbitch, which means "the valley of the demon", from where I could look down on my native hill and its Sleeping Hero. I saw from a vantage point of nineteen hundred feet, that I inhabited a mythic landscape, at the far side of which rose Moel Fammau. ["Hill of the Mothers": a sacred Welsh mountain.] The only thing about it that was English was the language of its present occupants.

As we went along the valley of the demon, my wife pointed out that the gateposts were too big, and shaped quite differently from the normal Pennine style, and many were of a different stone.

Then, high in the valley, and away from the single ruin of human habitation, first there was a well, built of stone, going down into the ground, with a collapsed roof; then we came to stones that had not been moved, and were pecked (worked by stone not metal), and the present evidence, which we are still collecting, is that it is a megalithic complex connected to a stellar cult, possibly of Orion.

But as I stood at the head of the valley next to a brook, my hand on an indisputable menhir, with a neat hole bored through it as if by a projectile, I thought: "And there the stone is, on the bank of the Bol-llyn river in Saltersffordd, and the hole through it. And thus begins this branch of the Mabinogi."

Let me tell you a story.

I set *The Owl Service* in the Mawddwy valley. This was because a friend of my wife had inherited Bryn Hall in Llanymawddwy. It had not been used as anything other than a holiday house since 1898, yet it was still looked on by the valley as the place where the people of power came. My wife's friend wanted the house to be used, and she offered it to us for a long holiday. The concept of *The Owl Service* had been with me for three years, but it had no context, until I saw the Bryn. I had to do the research, but here was the place.

The hall and its extensive grounds had been in the caring hands of Dafydd Rees Clocydd [bell ringer at church] since 1898, and, in 1962, he was still there.

For some reason, Dafydd took me as an added son. All the anecdotes and topographical stories in the novel are as he told them to me. And I have much more on tape. I never mentioned *The Mabinogion* to him, but said that I wanted to write a story about the valley.

For the rest of the valley, I was not so immediately acceptable, unless I was in Dafydd's company. I was staying in the house of the people of power, and assumptions were automatically made. We were ritualistically invited to visit the farms "for a cup of tea", and conversation was formal, stylised, polite and pre-ordained. I knew that I must obey the rule.

Then Mrs Jones Troed-y-Foel [Bottom-of-the-Hill] invited us. Her daughter had, that year, become Chief Harpist of Wales. After the cup of tea, the daughter was paraded before us, and I inwardly groaned, not least for her discomfort. She had been tricked out in a parody of Welsh costume that looked as though it had been bought at Woolworths, no doubt for the best of hospitable reasons, because that was what Saxons would expect to see in Wales. She sat at the harp, and she played.

And she could play. But all she played were the debased, over-decorated nineteenth-century hymns of the English idea of Welsh folk music. She finished. I thanked her, and praised, genuinely, her command of her harp. Then I said, "Do you know 'Gosteg yr Halen'?" [The oldest extant Welsh music.] She looked at me as if I had come from Mars. A Saxon. Asking that question. Knowing that the question was there to be asked.

It was then that she really played, her eyes closed. And she went on to play, and played again, but never in that "Welsh" costume. Later, she and her sister made tapes of penillion for me. From that question, "Do you know 'Gosteg yr Halen'?", the valley opened its door. That a Saxon should know the questions, and be interested to hear the answers, to show respect, while living in the house of the people of power, was incomprehensible, yet it was received as a compliment, and repaid in kind.

Nevertheless, it was Dafydd who led me through the writing of the book, and gave me, along with much else, an insight into the folk mind, which I have found applies everywhere, especially in my own family.

One day, Dafydd said that he had something to show me. He took me to a farm, and into a stone outbuilding. He pointed up. "See," he said, "my uncle made that. Good, isn't it?" I was looking at a superb example of a seventeenth-century queen-post roof of oak. I do not doubt that his uncle built it. But how many uncles ago?

The experience clarified what I already knew but had not voiced. The mind that has not been formally educated is not trapped in linear time. Memories of named individuals are identified for about three or four generations. Then the way is blocked, usually by a patriarch, beyond whom there is nothing, and to whom accrete tales and exploits of a giant. But I suspect that they are the accretions onto an individual of generations of history; for, beyond linear oral memory, we are in mythic time, where everything is simultaneously present; so that, for Dafydd, his uncle built the roof of the barn at the same time that the church where he and his father and grandfather rang the bell was built, and where the sexes are still segregated, and when Owain ab Gruffydd set up his parliament in Maengwyn Street in Machynlleth, at the same time as the Maen Llwyd [a megalith] was brought to the east of the town, and Gweli Tydecho [The Bed of Saint Tydecho: a rock slab] was slept in under Bwlch-y-Groes [The Pass of the Cross] and Tomen-y-Mur [Pigshit Wall] was home to the legions. And he is not wrong to think so.

The matter goes further. I was walking along a lane on a wet day when I found Dafydd, sack on shoulder, cap on head, sitting in the hedge. He was scratching a piece of slate with a pebble. He had written "Blodeuwedd". I asked what that was. "Just a name," said Dafydd, and threw the slate into the river. I broke my rule. "Was a man ever killed here?" I said. "Oh, yes," said Dafydd. "He was standing on the bank there. And a Red Indian shot him with an arrow from up on the Bryn, and the arrow went right through a stone and him. He must have escaped, the Indian, from Buffalo Bill's circus that was in Dolgelly that time. Funny, isn't it?"

No, it is not funny. It is illuminating. It explains the need for the onomastic element in folktale, legend and myth, to focus the content of the collective unconscious in the conscious, so that the story becomes actual for the people and for their place.

After *The Owl Service* had been published, Dafydd said that he wanted me to come to his house one night. "And bring your Missis for my Missis."

I went, with my wife, Griselda, whose job it was to keep Dafydd's wife occupied. Dafydd's wife had spent one week as a maid in Manchester Square, London, when she was a girl, and, as a result, she had never allowed Welsh to be spoken in her house.

Griselda took her off and began to admire the furniture. There was much to see: an anthropologist's doctorate lay here. For instance, a Queen Anne table, and on it a garish red plastic tomato that was a memory of a tea in Welshpool. Both were equally valued.

Dafydd sat me by the fire, and spoke softly. He said, "I think I shall close my eyes soon." It was a statement of intent, not a prognosis of an ailment. "When I am gone, my sons will sell what they can, and throw the rest in the river. You are to take the Beauty Things now, in case we do not meet again."

He reached up into the chimney and pulled down a soot-blackened set of horse brasses. They may have been made in Birmingham for tourists, but Dafydd had used them correctly: as apotropaic talismans; good luck insignia for a harvest; offerings to earth for breaking her. He explained the meaning of each to me. He carried them out of the house surreptitiously and into his shed.

There he assembled what I was to take into my stewardship: the broken gaff snapped in 1908 by the largest salmon ever to be seen in the Dovey; his grandmother's quern stone, which looks mediaeval; his father's worn and rusted adze head; an eighteenth-century mattock head, "which we used before They gave us spades"; a grindstone; a small, octagonal piece of limestone (for which Dafydd had no explanation, and had to pull out of the stones of his garden path); a circular laminated slate, lacking its gnomon, which was a seventeenth-century sun and moon dial that remains for me the highest expression of human optimism: a moon dial, correct for Cwm Cowarch.

And so on. The junk beyond price lay on the table. The Beauty Things. I was in tears. "Why me, Diobach?" He looked towards the house. "Because you hear. And your Welsh is better than my sons'."

I did not see Dafydd again. His sons sold what they could, and threw the rest in the river.

For thirty years I have kept faith with the Beauty Things. But I shall close my eyes in my turn. It is time for them to go. Is it possible, between you, to get them, as an entity, to a place that will be safe? And I have other memorabilia of Dafydd Rees Cilwern, Huw Halfbacon of *The Owl Service*, and hence Gwydion vab Don, of The Third Branch, magician, golden shoemaker, bard, smith, brother of Arianrhod, and father of Llew.

What, for him, were the essence of the Island of the Mighty, the essence of Being, must not be lost. Please, now you, take the Beauty Things.

15

Fierce Fires & Shramming Cold

I am illiterate: musically, that is; although I expect that there are many who would not think it necessary to add the qualification. Anyway, I can't read music; yet it has always been a necessity, in every aspect of life. I do not have a favourite piece of music, because that is an impossible concept, but, if I had, it would be *The Marriage of Figaro*.*

I listen. It is never a background, and I could not work if any were being played. And, though I have no favourite, I do tend to listen to the same piece over a long time, until something else takes its place.

I had just finished writing a film, Images, for an educational series, and the music that had coincided with that time was Benjamin Britten's "Serenade for Tenor and Horn". The combination of horn with the timbre of Peter Pears' voice was seductively lovely. It was the late morning of 16 April 1980, and I was listening to that record. In mid-phrase, everything changed. The horn and the voice were a threat, seductive still, but seducing me with death. I had to switch off quickly and get out of the room.

The next thing I remember is that I was standing in the kitchen, the sunlit kitchen, looking over a green valley with brook and trees; and the light was going out. I could see, but as if through a dark filter. And my solar plexus was numb.

Some contraption, a piece of mechanical junk left by one of the

* This lecture was delivered at an event organised by Stockport Health Care for World Mental Health Day at Stockport on 5 December 1996.

children, told me to pick it up. It was cylindrical and spiky, and had a small crank handle. I turned the handle. It was the guts of a cheap musical box, and it tinkled its few notes over and over again, and I could not stop. With each turn, the light dimmed and the feeling in my solar plexus spread through my body. When it reached my head, I began to cry with terror at the blankness of me, and the blankness of the world.

A scene from Eisenstein's "Alexander Nevsky" swamped my brain: the dreadful passage in which Nevsky dupes the Teutonic Knights onto the frozen lake, and the ice breaks, and their faceless armour takes them under. The cloaks float on the water before being pulled down, and the hands clutch at the ice floes, which flip over and seal in the knights.

All that helplessness, cold and horror comprised me. I was alone in the house, and throughout the afternoon I turned the tinkle tinkle tinkle of the broken toy, which became the sound of the ice. My body was as heavy as the armour and the waterlogged cloaks as I slid beneath the ice.

When the family came home, I was lying on the kitchen settle, in a foetal position, without moving or speaking, until I went to bed at midnight. Sleep was unconsciousness without rest until the morning, when I had to face what I now dreaded: the camera and the crew, and speaking for five days into an unblinking lens to communicate with the millions of people on the other side of it, to generate emotional energy for them from my dead heart.

I was incapable of emotion except that of being incapable of emotion. I had no worth. I poisoned the planet. I noticed, but did not wonder at how the finished film showed none of this. I knew that the man was me, but I did not know him.

The following year, Images won the First Prize at the Chicago International Film Festival; but by that time I had spent twelve months of twelve hours each day on the settle, my face to the wall, waiting only for the twelve hours in bed. My small children would, instinctively, stroke the back of my neck, not speaking. Their stroking was the only thing that reached me.

The doctor diagnosed "endogenous depression", which meant depression without external cause, and prescribed, progressively, the pharmacopoeia of antidepressants. None of them worked. For two years I lay either in the kitchen or in bed. There was no feeling except of a wretched superfluity. I was the grape skin after the harvest; and even that gave me the weight of reality I did not feel.

Then, one morning, almost two years to the day, I woke to find that I had come back. It was instant. Nothing was wrong. What had all the fuss been about?

Two events followed, almost coincidentally. My doctor, who was a fine doctor, retired and a younger partner took me on. And I had a long letter, with a longer c.v. attached, from a Dr Kay Redfield Jamison, Associate Professor at the Neuropsychiatric Insitute Center for the Health Sciences at the University of California, Los Angeles, to ask whether I was willing to take part in a survey of mood disorders and patterns of creativity in "eminent" British writers and artists. Her criterion of choice was that the participants should have won at least one prestigious award in their field. I agreed to try, noting to myself that the prolific intensity of the c.v. suggested that the doctor knew from personal experience more than she was saying.

A familial connection between mental illness and creativity had been suggested by other surveys. But Dr Jamison's structure of questioning enabled her to elicit more precise facts. The protocol I had to fill in was a thoroughgoing grilling, and took several days to complete. And the subsequent analysis of the data was more than significant.

In brief: 38 per cent of writers and of artists had been treated for a mood disorder, of whom 75 per cent had had antidepressants or lithium prescribed, or had been hospitalized. For poets, the figure was 50 per cent on lithium. 63 per cent of playwrights had been treated for depression, and more than half through psychotherapy. 89 per cent of the survey, including all novelists and poets, reported periods of high productivity, lasting usually betwen two and four weeks, and extending into most other areas of living.

Dr Jamison knew exactly what questions to ask, thereby producing an overall response much more detailed and informative than I have outlined. In her summary, with grave understatement, she said that the percentage of treatment was "extremely high", since the prevalence rates for manic-depressive and depressive illness, in the general population, are 1 per cent and 5 per cent respectively.

For a complete understanding of the implications, I would recommend the book she went on to write, which incorporated the British survey: *Touched With Fire: Manic-Depressive Illness and the Artistic Temperament* (The Free Press, New York, 1994).

At least I was not alone. And, with greater understanding and hindsight, I could see that the whole of my life had had a pre-echoing pattern, at a low level, of mania and inertia. But why had this pattern become without an apparent trigger a full-blown state of near-catatonia and wretchedness, in the form of cold self-loathing for me, and desperation for my family? I was soon to find out.

Fourteen months after returning to "normality", yet without any ideas that had enabled me to work, I was hit as unexpectedly by the most demanding task of my life, so far: work that occupied me, at full stretch, without a diminution of energies, for two months short of twelve years. I was firing on all cylinders, including many I did not know I had. The stress, though different, was no further from the unendurable, either for me or for the family, than the two-year dark. But it was exciting and it was positive. And that gave me a clue, or at least a model. I had had to be totally incapacitated, in order to build the energy, to fill the reservoir, that would be needed. The analogy with an enforced hibernation fitted. If I could live with this self-loathing, and see it as a signal to let the waters rise, it could remain a necessary though unpleasant part of a positive and creative process. As long as that thought stayed, I could endure.

There were tough periods during the first six years, at irregular intervals, but not the bottomless pit. I kept going. And they lasted hours, days, but not often weeks. The importance lay, as I faced the wall from the settle, in knowing that: a) this would pass. b) there was nothing I could do, so I should go with its purpose. c) it would also, having passed, return. d) it would pass.

In 1989, after six years of working and living on this unstable raft, I sensed the ice floes tinkle again, in the distance. I also realised, and wondered why the importance of it had not struck me, that none of the antidepressants had ever worked. So I took myself off to the doctor and gave him this fresh insight. He asked me to tell him in detail the rhythms of my work patterns, checked through the encyclopaedia of my medical notes, relating the two, and said, "There has been a misdiagnosis. You are clearly manic-depressive." It remains the best news that I have ever heard.

To anyone who is in any way ill, let me assure you that there is nothing that brings greater relief and solace, no matter what is wrong, than an accurate diagnosis. With that weapon, you can act on the wisest medical advice in the world, given by the first century Roman, Persius: *Venienti occurite morbo*: "Don't muck about: hit disease head on."

That is why Montgomery kept the portrait of Rommel with him all the time: to learn the man. To know is to respect and not to fear. I found myself walking out of a doctor's surgery almost weeping with euphoria that, at last, I knew that I was wading in the shallows of psychosis. Where did the continental shelf end? Where was the abyss? I should learn to take soundings.

I remembered the analogy of enforced hibernation. It could be made more positive; it could be moved further and be interpreted as a chance to incubate ideas. Then a line of Theodore Roethke (himself a manic-depressive) appeared: "In a dark time, the eye begins to see."

With a speed that I could hardly keep up with, the whole was revealed. (What happened, incidentally, is a typical example of manic connection, of "finding". It was as if a computer were cross-referring its files.)

I had been here before, at Oxford, as a Classicist. From that I saw the universality of the personal. It was the ancient, mystical experience of "black sight". Prophets are often blind. Oracular caves, where vatic priests go to find truths that cannot be found in the light, are a part of our history. That history, which is the history on which all Western thought is based, is Classical Greek. What we call logic may just as well be defined as "the way adult Athenian males of the fifth century BC think". Yet Greek culture and art (especially the tragic theatre), which we perceive to be the height of human achievement, descends from the worship of Dionysos, whose epithet was in Greek "*mainomonos*", "raving mad", and the theatre started as his temple, where illusion was the reality. A modern definition of madness is the taking of illusion for reality. The Greeks sat in the temple of their mad god and, for a while, watched illusion as reality. To behave so is madness. Herodotus reported that the Scythians blamed the Greeks for the introduction of insanity to the world, since it was not an act of reason to adopt a god who drives humans mad.

So we have a fascinating paradox, where the source of our criteria for stability of thought is built on a culture that appears to have based itself on the worship of madness, while this same *mainomenos* Dionysos also represented indomitable life. In Classical Greek there are two words for life. One is "*bios*", which means simply life, or a life. The other is "*zoe*", which is the eternal life force. To have "*zoe*" associated with "*mainomenos*" could not be more instructive.

Later, it seems that Christ built into his ministry metaphors and rituals taken straight from the cult of Dionysos that flourished amongst non-Greeks between the lake of Genesareth and the Phoenician coast, which he would have come to know, if he did not know already, on his journey to Tyre. Which is again instructive, and may legitimately lead to an hypothesis.

To look at Christ the man, removed from his divinity, which is how most of the world sees him, leaves little to the imagination or to prejudice. A Jew, for instance, recognises him as an inspired Rabbi; but a psychiatrist, at the same time, has to suspect the symptoms, since a strand running through almost everything recorded of that ministry, psychologically and physically, could be seen as an account of manic-depression. Only his divinity set him apart; and there he may have modelled the imagery on raving Dionysos.

I am aware that what I am saying may be surprising to many and obnoxious to some. But the link cannot be easily avoided. In Minoan Crete, where the worship of Dionysos arose, his name, "*Dios nusos*", meant "Son of God". He was a god who suffered, and triumphed over suffering. And a clue to the connection with Christ may be found as late as AD 691, when the Second Council of Constantinople decreed that wine treaders should be forbidden their traditional cry of "Dionysos!" and must replace it with "*Kyrie eleison!*" Walter Otto, in considering the Greek word "*mania*" in connection with Dionysos, called it a visionary attempt to explain a state in which the vital powers of Man are enhanced to the limit, in which consciousness and the unconscious merge to a breakthrough, which he equated with "the Dionysian", and I recognise as "creativity".

There is a deal more to be said, but let this stand for all.

Jesus could, by making much of Psalm 80, and by reference to the Septuagint Jeremiah, if he knew it (God to Israel: "Yet I planted thee a chosen vineyard."), have claimed Biblical authority and fulfilment for what he said and did, as happens so often in the

Gospels. And, by taking the symbolism of wine, equating it with his blood, and referring to himself as "the true vine" (John 15.1 ff), he was likening himself to the Dionysos that we know through the Orphic texts. He may even have tried to usurp him.

The peculiar story of Christ's cursing of the fig tree out of season, recorded in Mark 11, has puzzled Biblical commentators. A plausible argument, given the Bible's constant use of metaphor, is that Christ was privy to the Dionysiac Mysteries, the climax of which was the removal from the sacrificial goat, in great secrecy, of an organ called "the heart", "*kradiē*" in Ionic Greek, and its preservation in a basket. It was not the heart that was removed but the phallos, and so sacred was this act that it could be mentioned only obliquely and by punning. "*Kradē*" is the Greek for "fig"; and in a myth of Dionysos he makes a ritual phallos by carving a fig branch. Hence the profound pun, "*kradiē*" and "*kradē*", of the Mysteries.

Also, but here the modern novelist may be at work (although the commentators have no more credible answer), a further instance can be seen in John 1.48, where Nathanael is perplexed that Jesus should have recognised him. Christ's apparently meaningless reply, "When thou wast under the fig tree, I saw thee," could have been an encoded, "I remember you from when we were both at a celebration of Dionysos." The Mediterranean wine culture was the common concrete background to two divergent realities: the founding of Christianity and everything that can be subsumed under the term "Dionysian Mystery". Such an initial convergence would be seen as a threat by the early Church.

On no account should it be thought that I am seeking to undermine a religion, or that I should want to criticise faith. The opposite is the case. If my hypothesis were ever found to be fact, I should hold that Christianity had been strengthened, not diminished. A tenet of the Church is that God entered History by becoming Man. If that were to be a truth, I have said nothing outlandish. If Christ was Man, he was of his own will open to all of Man's experiences, even unto death. There can be no dispensations. I should not want my god to be unable to understand me and my experience; but I am unequivocally and emphatically not saying, "Manic-depression means God. Hallelujah."

The most poetic aspect of all, for me, is that the first word of the oldest complete sentence to have survived in the West is "madness". The opening line of the *Iliad* is an invocation to the goddess to sing the fury of Achilles; and the word used is *menin*, which relates to the outward loss of control through the mind's insanity.

The road we travel could scarcely be longer.

Meanwhile, Dr Jamison has co-authored, with Fredrick K. Goodwin, the definitive, nine hundred and thirty-eight page exegesis: *Manic-Depressive Illness* (OUP, 1990), which, to her other multiple honours and academic qualifications, added the Most Outstanding Book in Biomedical Sciences, chosen by the Association of American Publishers; while I have undertaken the *via dolorosa* of arriving at the correct level of lithium carbonate for my body, the only drug to control manic-depression.

From here onwards I must be careful to differentiate between the personal and the general, because manic-depression is only a simple label for a complex and varied condition. It took Kay Jamison nine hundred and thirty-eight pages to deal with it, and here I am just trying to be helpful. My only qualification for speaking is that I have found ways to live a profitable life with a most dangerous and, so far, incurable condition, and I have read the literature.

Kay Jamison found that there was a tendency for creative minds to refuse to continue with lithium. The freedom from the "lows" did not compensate for the loss of the "highs". So it was with me. There was no stress, no grief, no animation, no laughter, no thought, no ideas. I was socially safe and could be taken anywhere. I stopped work. I had no interests. It was unique, for me, and I translated it as, "If this is what normality is, give me back my madness." I refused to continue with the lithium treatment.

If it had not been for something else, the result could have been almost anything. I may never know. However, I started work again, and the final six years of the novel involved me entirely in anthropology: the embracing of the philosophy and thought patterns of a highly sophisticated so-called primitive society. For our purposes, all I need say is that one of their models is that the cosmos is built of nine temporal dimensions, all capable of being simultaneously present.

Coming to terms with the demands of this society, especially after my training in formal logic and Hellenistic thought, took up my concentration, and it was about four years into the discipline that I became consciously aware that I had had no manic-depressive episodes.

That is not strictly true. At one level, I go through the cycle every twenty-four hours, but that level is low. All my life, my metabolism has made me severely dysfunctional in the morning. I take a long time to wake up, and feel rotten, and can't think. But also, now, every morning, in the middle of the gloom, I go through a depression. It is slight, and normally lasts minutes. But it can threaten worse, so I always check, with a measure of my own devising.

I am amazed, and delighted, that one of the stone flags of the kitchen floor has the fossil footprints of a small dinosaur on its surface. When I feel myself entering the blackness, I look at the footprints. If my reaction is still of awe ("How terrific to have this frozen moment of two hundred million years ago still active!") then I know that the blackness is a railway bridge flicker, not a tunnel. If the reaction is a panicky: "How can you bear not to be able to move for two hundred million years?" I take that as a warning, and apply one of the "primitive" mental exercises that are concerned with the handling of time. I side-step, as it were, the blackness.

The method can be adapted to any place or circumstance. It is personal to me, but I feel that it should be examined medically, to discover what is behind the metaphor, in case there is something potentially of general value.

I am by no means complacent. Manic-depression is devious, in that it is not always a cyclical or wave-like phenomenon. To hit "low" when "high" can be fatal. The greatest threat in manic-depression is of suicide. A quarter to a half of sufferers are going to kill themselves, if something is not done.

I have always had the strongest philosophical, social and ethical objections to suicide. And, even at my worst, suicide has never offered itself as the way to help either me or the rest of the world. It is a particularly vile act, because it loads friends and relatives, the closest, the most dear, with a sense of guilt that cannot easily be assuaged, each one thinking that they must be personally responsible for what the suicide has done; and this frequently triggers mental breakdowns, alcoholism and further suicide through the generations, since manic-depression is genetic. Its pattern is clear, through my maternal line, for a hundred and fifty observable years, though never diagnosed until now. Usually, we have been "under the doctor with nerves".

Even now I know that I can never drop my guard. I have too much to do, for one thing, and my greatest concern is to help bring about the future. I am not here to kill it.

Manic-depression can ambush. It can hit when least expected. Most sufferers know that, and take precautions. Winston Churchill, for instance, always stood as far away as possible from the edge of a railway platform. I try never to be out of instant reach of a sympathetic mind. There is something of a joke here. I am by nature a loner. I find my own company stimulating. I abhor cities, crowds and social events. I seek the isolation of woods and hills. My work of necessity is isolate. Yet I try, when indoors especially, never to be out of reach of the safety that one human being, who need not be in the same room, secures.

It is particularly important when I am drawing on the enormous energies provided by a "high" in order to sustain a piece of work; so that, when I finish, or pause, if the rebound of a "low" were to meet the remains of a "high", I could distract, or adjust, my emotions by having a fragment of "normality" to refer to. The end of a book, and the end of a lecture, are the times of greatest need. So much for me. Now, is there anything I can say about this chameleon madness that is of general use? I shall try. First, let me speak to the family.

The most important hurdle to be crossed before any progress can be made is for the family, and particularly the sufferer, to acknowledge the illness and to seek, and follow, medical advice. Then, do not let the sufferer (despite my example) give up on the treatment without your fighting, and do report the matter. It is almost diagnostic that a manic-depressive, once the agony is mediated, will react with a feeling of omnipotent well-being, and insist that a cure has taken place. There is no cure.

Never, at any time or under any stress, lose patience and say something to the effect of: "Why don't you pull yourself together?" Learn, and keep before you, so that you will recognise why you cannot even begin to realise what the other is experiencing, Gerard Manley Hopkins' lines from his poem "No worst, there is none":

> . . . mind has mountains; cliffs of fall,
> Frightful, sheer, no-man-fathomed. Hold them cheap
> May who ne'er hung there.

Hold them cheap, may who ne'er hung there. He is saying, because he knew, that only the manic-depressive can truly understand the manic-depressive. Accept that you cannot feel what the other feels; that your sympathy will, no matter how great, be taken to the edge of breaking. It is here that sympathy and empathy must be most clearly differentiated between, and here you cannot empathise.

Remember that everyone in the equation will be touched by it, and do not hesitate to go for help on your own account. It may be a unique event for you, but it will not be for the doctor.

There is a paradox that is so easy to miss that I must stress it here. I may have spent a disproportionate time on the experience of depression, because it is then that the individual is in most pain, which is hard for the family to stand by and watch in a feeling of helplessness. But there is a worse helplessness for the family, and that, strangely, is the "high", not the "low", since the sufferer is so energetic, so persuasive and persuaded, that there is no appealing to reason, and the family, in self-defence, must close ranks, or, inevitably, be ground down.

Contrariwise, if there is reason and it can be appealed to, then everyone may share in the excitement, because the "high" could have produced something new, good, and true. It is all a matter of balance.

To the manic-depressive, I would say: don't try to deceive yourself, nor feel sorry for yourself. Apply what I have said to the family to your point of view. Stick with the treatment. Devise your own defensive and diagnostic measures, the equivalent of my dinosaur footprints, if you are able. Listen to your family, even if you have to preface what they say with: "they don't know what they're talking about, but I'm big enough to humour them". Then keep your word, and humour them. You are not alone. You have worth. You are loved. There is help.

Let me end by taking a longer perspective. It is an interesting question whether, from a Darwinian point of view, manic-depressives evolved, and, if so, why; and an even more interesting question why they are not extinct. Our son, who is a postgraduate biologist, has suggested, in what he would call a "coffee-time" idea, that an answer may lie in the fact that we are still savannah apes. Since a significant proportion of manic-depressives have creative minds, and are dominant when "high", evolution would select for them, because they would be likely to have made their innovative contribution, and to have bred, before their condition became fatal.

If you have seen the film 2001, you will remember the ape picking up a bone and looking at it, this way, then that way; turning his head, this way, then that way. His eyes light up as he sees the connection. He is the inventor of the first tool. In a moment of elation, he throws the bone into the air. As it revolves it becomes a space vessel. We may have seen the first manic-depressive. And if he has reproduced before this moment it is biologically acceptable for him to die now.

It is frequently observed that innovators have been manic-depressive. A common retort, and one that applies to me, is that innovators do not "think". They create by "seeing" involuntarily, and only then refine the creation by thought. For me, a novel is a series of connections which have always existed, but which no one else has seen.

The fortunate manic-depressive, in this way, invents a device that benefits humanity, discovers a cure (perhaps, one day, for manic-depression, should that be desirable), or creates a work of art. The unfortunate manic-depressive "sees" as does the fortunate; but it is not a true connection, and there is not available, in the degree of insanity, the logic to think out not the refinement but the absurdity. The connection then is more likely to be: "I shall buy two hundred lawnmowers, and shall have solved the problem of global warming."

The differences are so slight. If you alone can see the "truth", you need good friends who understand that you have "knowledge that is sad to have to know".

The worst case I have come across is that of an American psychiatrist, who was so successful in his accurate, intuitive and non-rational insights, that a special faculty was set up for his work. Shortly afterwards, he became ill, and was diagnosed as manic-depressive. How, then, could he himself trust his intuitive genius? And how were the admiring colleagues who had gathered around this great man to react to his hunches in the future?

I am only a writer, a maker of dreams. You can dismiss me and no harm is done. If I were your lawyer, or your bank manager, it would have been imprudent of me to have spoken today.

Kay Jamison, however, now Professor of Psychiatry at the Johns Hopkins University School of Medicine, having established her position as world authority on manic-depression, sits at her desk, takes up her pen, and writes *An Unquiet Mind: a Memoir of Moods and Madness* (Knopf, New York, 1995; Picador, London, 1996), which is a detailed and uncompromising account of her life-long dialogue with her own experience of relentless manic-depression. It is the bravest, and the most hopeful, document that I have ever read.

It made me, after sixteen years, dare to put on that record of "Serenade for Tenor and Horn", and to listen.

16

The Voice that Thunders

The end of a book tends to write itself. What I have to do is to sit, breathe and make the marks on the paper. Then, with exponential speed, it is: last page, last paragraph, last sentence, last line, last letter; full stop.*

I placed the full stop of *Strandloper*, looked at my watch, and wrote: "14.30. Tuesday. 25 April. 1995." Then I went back to the full stop, and thought: Why didn't I put just that in the first place? What I had undergone had all been in order to reach a full stop. The point was the point.

I had set off for it by deciding to do something useful on a hot day. I had brought up from the files a box I use for newspaper cuttings that I keep in case any of them should provoke an idea in the future, and started to cull the redundant. I chid myself for having amassed so much dross for my magpie mind. Then I stopped, and read and re-read an item from the *Congleton Chronicle*, our local newspaper, of November 1977. I must have read the article before, otherwise it would not have been in the box, yet I had no memory of it, while now it burnt my brain.

It was a brief article, recording the story of a twenty-year-old bricklayer, William Buckley, from my neighbouring hamlet of Marton, who had been transported for life to New Holland in 1803, had escaped into the bush, survived, and had lived for thirty-two years as an Aborigine before joining a party of prospecting Englishmen in order to prevent their massacre, as a result of which

* This lecture was delivered at The Royal Festival Hall, London, on 7 July 1996.

he was given a free pardon. The article was headed: "The Wild Man of Marton". I looked at my watch, and noted: "14.30. Tuesday. 21 June. 1983. William Buckley".

So it began. Why had something, presented as amusing and trivial, taken up precisely four thousand, three hundred and twenty-six days of my life and produced a novel at an average rate of 14.1 words a day, or approximately 0.5875 words an hour? There are two answers. The first is that it had been the most rewarding and demanding period of my life so far. The second is that I had no choice. I did not even have to defend myself by hiding behind Hazlitt's statement that: "If a man leaves behind him any work which is a model of its kind, we have no right to ask whether he could do anything else, or how he did it, or how long he was about it."

I am going to try to communicate something of this experience, despite Hazlitt.

The first question that has to be asked may be phrased as: why subject oneself to the ordeal of constructing a work of fiction? The answer is that the world is messy, and the truth hard to find in its tangled thickets. Truth is best found by the writer's taking the facts, pruning them, and then arranging what is left into the simplest possible pattern. This necessitates a degree of fabrication, which presents us with the paradox that the writer has to manipulate the facts in order to make what is essential clear and true. At its most extreme, reality can be expressed in art most accurately as myth. And, as I progressed into *Strandloper*, I became aware that the historical William Buckley's life matched the elements of the mythic Quest.

There was no altruism in what I was doing. Writers, at the point of writing, in the preparation for writing, in the act of writing, are the most selfish of beings. They have no social concern. Only their obsession matters, and you interrupt a writer then at your peril.

So a better question is: what makes some people, regardless of cost to themselves and others, write at all? Subjectively, it is merely something that has to be done. Plato set poets, of which he was one, at the top of his hit list, against the day when he could establish his ideal state. And the world authority in her field, the American psychiatrist, Kay Redfield Jamison, has made the grotesque discovery, in her surveys of writers, and of creativity in the arts, the military professions and those of business, that some 50 per cent of the significant innovators suffer from a lethal psychosis, lethal because of its 50 per cent suicide risk, which is largely ignored by society since its occurrence in the general public is not more than 1 per cent.

The last impression I want to make is one of angst or gloom. The brain is too clever for that. The main drive is what C. S. Lewis cunningly calls "joy", and it is in finding that "joy" that the brain is at its most clever.

I am happiest when engaged in establishing and pursuing research.

In order to make sense, it is time for me to say a little of how I write: not how to write: just how I write. I'll use *Strandloper*, since it's the nearest to my experience.

I count as my main asset the combination of an academic's and a magpie's mind that sees, finds or makes connections and patterns where others do not. Also essential to creativity is the ability to doodle mentally and to play.

I read a newspaper cutting about a curious fellow from Marton. I know instantly that I am pregnant with his story. I look at the story, and make a list of primary subjects that I shall have to know about in great detail before I can begin; and they will each consist of separate fibres, as in a rope, which will unwind and have to be followed in their turn, as I progress. The fibres will have fibres.

Here is the academic at work. I must learn all there is to be known. I grow a bibliography. I read and read, and take notes, books of notes. And this is the joy that leads me on. I am learning what I did not know, and unlike purely academic work, the subjects appear not to be linked. For instance: mediaeval English stained glass; the system of convict transport in the nineteenth century; neurological disturbance of the optic nerve and its cultural significance. And that is only a fraction. The magpie is gratified by the collecting; and the writer is enthralled as the unconnected themes begin to converge, apparently of their own accord (although I am aware of the more mundane theory of selective perception) and for me it is the convergence, an elegant and natural simplicity of resolution, that hidden union, which has always been waiting: the numinous as a book.

The point cannot be reached by the academic element, which is a drudge. There comes a moment when all has been read. The intellect then has to be suppressed, because I can't "think" something into being. That is the job of the subconscious. It shows, and tells, so that I "see", and "dream", and "hear", and "find". I am the sophisticated word processor and the first reader. Thereafter the intellect is freed to edit what the subconscious has written.

Before I say more of William Buckley, I should put the culling of the files into perspective. It was the Summer Solstice of 1983. The last piece of original work that I had written, *The Stone Book Quartet*, was finished in the summer of 1977. Six years had gone by in silence. There had been nothing to add. "When may we expect the next novel?" said my publisher of the day. "When it's ready," I said, and got on with not writing.

Fortunately for my nervous system, I had never given much credence to the phenomenon of "writer's block". I was more inclined to think of it as "writer's impatience", and to follow Arthur Koestler's dictum: "Soak; and wait." With *The Stone Book Quartet*, I had emptied my well, and nothing could be done until the water table was restored. And that is where I was at the Summer Solstice of 1983, until 2.30 p.m., when the well became a gusher.

My first problem was to find William Buckley. (He was said to

have been born in 1780, and brought up by his grandfather.)
I searched the decayed parish registers. There was no record of
him. Then a voice, which many writers learn to heed, said:
"Bishop's Transcripts". At the period in question, and for centuries
before that, the priest of a parish was obliged not only to keep his
registers but each year to make a copy and to send it to the
Bishop's Palace. By the end of the eighteenth century, the provision
of a Bishop's Transcript had become patchy. One nearby incumbent
of Marton kept the actual registers themselves in a bag by his chair,
the easier to light his pipe with the spills that he made from them.
So, as I sat in the County Record Office in Chester, contemplating
the pile of uncatalogued sheets that the archivist had brought from
the vaults, I was not optimistic.

The baptisms of the Transcript were there for 1782. They were
identical to those of the register, with one additional entry.
"William, son of Eliza Buckley, March 31st." And, in the margin,
in another hand, "Illigitim". The County Record Office reeled, as
I involuntarily yelled: "Oh, William!"

The next part was easy, now that the clew was in my hand. Eliza
was the teenage daughter of Jonathan Buckley, and she had an
older brother William, after whom to name a son. The following
day I was in the John Rylands Library of Manchester University,
which holds the archive of the Marton estate. Within minutes
I had identified Jonathan Buckley's farm, such as it was (one acre,
three roods and thirty perches of bits of scattered land) from the
rent books and maps, and the subsequent change of the house into
a school.

I had to see inside the house, to feel where William had grown
up, to stand in the room from which he had gone out to spend
thirty-two years as an Aborigine. I stooped under the beams.
William had been measured at 6 feet 5 7/8 inches tall in 1835. The
headroom in the transport ship in which he had spent six months
chained in darkness, with no sight of the sun, had been 5 feet 7

inches, below the beams. By the end of it all, I felt that I knew the inside of William Buckley very well, simply by inference from what I found he had experienced.

But still I had to look into Buckley eyes. I had identified his closest living relative, Arthur Buckley. I was warned that he was old, ill, reclusive, depressed and bad tempered. I went to the house at Fiddler's Elbow, where he had been born and lived all his life. I knocked on the door. Silence. I was about to knock again when I heard a slow and distant shuffling. The shuffling came closer. I felt my adrenaline pumping. Any moment now I was going to be as near as it was possible to be to William Buckley. I was going to see into the gene pool.

There was a drawing of bolts, the door opened an inch. I made out a blue eye behind thick lenses, and a spike of uncombed silver hair. That was all.

Then I did a stupid thing. I entered on a preamble.

"Mr Buckley?"

Grunt.

"I'm sorry to bother you, but I wonder if you could spare me a few minutes. I'd like to talk to you."

"I don't think so," said a toneless voice, and the door began to close.

Desperate, I said: "My name's Alan Garner." I had been going to say, "I'm a writer, and I'm working on a book about your family," or something like that. The door was pulled wide, and Arthur Buckley said, "You're Colin's lad! Come in! Come in! I know more about Garners than you do!" And I had come in order to know more about Buckleys than he did.

He beckoned me into the kitchen with his head. He walked with difficulty and never let go of his trousers. "Sit thi down. Tek thi bacca." He welcomed me formally, and eased himself into the only armchair. I fetched a stool from the table. He was agitated with pleasure, and I looked into an alert William Buckley as he told me how in the Twenties and Thirties, he had, with his family and mine, made up the local brass band. It had been the centre of his life. Along the length of the mantelpiece were curled and time-coloured photographs of the band in uniform, with their instruments, fat Big Bill Garner in the middle, holding his baton.

Arthur Buckley talked obsessively, reliving the great days; but I noticed that, even sitting, he kept one hand on his trousers. I asked him what was wrong.

"Me braces snapped last week."

"Haven't you another pair?"

"No. There's a strap for cases somewhere in the back bedroom, but I can't get up the stairs."

I found the strap. Arthur Buckley staggered against the mantelpiece, while I stood behind, trying to hold him upright, as I tied the strap twice round.

It went through my head: if only would-be Doctors of Philosophy, who write to me asking for opinions on my work and its relationship to structualism, deconstructualism, phenomenology, semiotics, reductionism, with special reference to subplot, after-plot, subvocalisation, not forgetting metacognition, if they could only see that writing lies more in trying to keep an old man's trousers up and that from such moments is born a *Strandloper*.

Arthur Buckley was tired. It was time to go. I said that I'd enjoyed our talk very much.

"Ay," said Arthur Buckley. "We've had us a grand crack."

I had to be away for a few days, and I asked him whether I could come and talk again the following week.

"If I'm here," he said. "Then I'll tell you the truth about Maurice Garner."

Finally I asked him whether he would let me take some photographs of him. He agreed, and I took a series of close-up portraits. That is another pattern of my research. In framing the photograph I ask basic questions of the subject; and when I look into someone's eyes through a lens I see something more than with my eye alone.

We parted in good cheer. When I went back a few days later Arthur Buckley was dead. I still do not know the truth about Maurice Garner, but I had gained much of the truth about William Buckley. I knew him now.

The rest of the English section of the book, and the transportation to Australia, presented no irresolvable problems. I had to follow the lines of the pattern. Then came alarm. The lines were there and flowing; yet they were starting to approach and to interact with other lines, a pattern I had dealt with in *The Stone Book Quartet*. The cross-references were unavoidable. *The Stone Book Quartet* had been written as a sequel to *Strandloper*, beginning nine years before *Strandloper* was conceived. That inner voice which instructs but will not discuss, told me not to hesitate. So I put my disconcertion aside, and obeyed. I continued to pursue the Lewisian "joy".

What can be said to have been among the qualities of *Strandloper*, to compensate for the difficulties, is that it has been a joyous work in its making. Everybody I have approached has been friendly, and eager to help. But beware. I warned against involvement with writers. The ruthlessness can take many forms; and I should tell you that, whenever you are in the presence of a writer, anything you say will be taken down, and it will be used. The difference with *Strandloper* is that the victims have not merely acquiesced. They have shared in the joy.

What happens is that the writer, either having written a paragraph, or about to start one, feels that something extra is needed, something slight, a seasoning more than an ingredient. These seasonings cannot be invented. They have to be stolen. They make all the difference, changing a text from adequate to inspired.

A new butcher moved to our nearby village, which has an enclave of insecure upwardly mobile, executives. They expect servility, not only civility, from shopkeepers. To help him at weekends, the butcher employs Raymond, a retired colleague, who was the apprentice of my father's best friend. I had not seen Raymond for nearly fifty years, but the first time I went into the shop we spontaneously broke into a loud exchange of improvised sexual verbal abuse and scatology, lowering the executive tone, all in broad dialect. I saw the young butcher's eyes flicker in alarm. Bad for business.

"Give over," said Raymond. "I've known our Alan since his bum were as big as me shirt button."

Within half an hour it was in the book, making a crucial scene not just sorrowful, but searingly human.

Nicknames cannot be improvised, either. All the nicknames of *Strandloper* are of local men, delivered mostly by the stonemason, Ken. His one misgiving is that Eggy Mo, an innocent in the book, a near-psychopath in reality, may not be the illiterate he is said to be.

Taxi driver, John, used to be a coalman, after his father, and so, inevitably in Cheshire, is known as Cobby. I asked him whether he would mind if I "borrowed" him. He was so amused that he told me a rhyme long known in his family.

> Owd Cob and Young Cob and Young Cob's son.
> Young Cob's Owd Cob when Owd Cob's done.

He was giving me more than he knew. In Cheshire dialect, "Cobby" is a coalman. But "Cob" is chief man, governor of a gang, leader. This was so important that the rhyme not only went into the dialogue, but shifted the structure of the book, and gave the name to one of its sections. It expressed the inexpressible, in particular at one cathartic resolution of an Aboriginal acceptance of the pain of what had to be to achieve the purpose of a life. All from asking an ex-coalman if I could use his name, which I did, as well as the rhyme.

A last example: I needed an opening for the first chapter of the transport to Australia, something memorable, poetic, yet indicative of a destroyed mind. The text reads: "I chases 'em; I flaps my apron at 'em. But they sees me coming. They sees my apron. But I'll get 'em. One day." It is all the character ever says, but he says it for six months.

The fragmentation, and the rhythm, enabled me to create whole scenes in the smallest space, by using single phrases or sentences impressionistically to show the duration of the voyage, even to its being used for the commital of the man's corpse to the sea.

In our son's first term at New College, Oxford, he was sitting by the lake with three friends, watching the ducks, when out of the bushes ran a scout, a college servant, making for the ducks, shouting: "I chases 'em; I flaps my apron at 'em. But they sees me coming. They sees my apron. But I'll get 'em. One day."

Nobody is safe. I was lucky. All whom the thieving magpie robbed, delight in the private joke. *Strandloper* is as much a novel made by a community as by an individual.

The original reason for my turning out my files at that Summer Solstice was that I was too exhausted to do anything else. I had spent six weeks travelling 46,000 miles, to lecture in Canada, the United States and Australia.

The Australian visit had been arranged by my closest friend, who has given me the sobriquet of "manky academic" instead of *academic manqué*. He is Professor (now Emeritus) Ralph Elliott, a descendant of Martin Luther, nephew of Nobel Laureate Max Born, and cousin to Ben Elton and to Olivia Newton John, and then Master of University House at the Australian National University in Canberra. His speciality is runic inscriptions, in which he is the acknowledged ultimate authority, and an internationally respected scholar of Old and Middle English, especially of Chaucer and the Gawain poet, and of the works of Thomas Hardy.

We met because he wrote to me to tell me that I must be the first writer since the fourteenth century to use the same dialect and landscape in my writing as the Gawain poet had used in Sir *Gawain and the Green Knight*. And we had, from different backgrounds and disciplines, arrived at the same answer in identifying the location of the Green Chapel.

We are also concerned in the nature of The Matter of Britain and the need for it to be kept alive by its working and reworking. For me, *Strandloper* is *Sir Gawain and the Green Knight*. The elements of The Matter of Britain are in both.

It was vital that I had seen Australia, seen its light and hues, smelt its smells, heard its sounds. Without them, it would have been an insult to dare the quest. The other ingredient, without which it would not have started, was the tireless generosity of Ralph Elliott and his position that gave him access to the libraries and archives of Australia. He had the means to dig out and photo-copy rare books, unique books, diaries, notes, sketches, letters: all the paraphernalia of the land that was to become William Buckley's.

Ralph himself is a William Buckley. He left Germany as a teenager, one step ahead of the SS, to come to Britain, knowing three words of English. His mother told him that it was necessary to know only two in order to get by in that benighted land: "Corned beef" and "Darling". His cousin said that, with one more word, he would be entirely at ease among the British. All he had to say, frequently, was "Bugger". Thus armed, Ralph set out from the chapel at mid-night, pricking o'er the plain, to develop a career devoted to the enlightenment of the English language around the world.

So, for Australian documentary research, I had my mole. His most outrageous feat was to send me a photocopy of the only book to describe in detail the physical culture of the Aborigines of the area where William Buckley spent his thirty-two years: nine hundred and seventy-eight pages, by express airmail letter post.

In such ways, I was kept secure and happy in the research. I had all the external facts I needed. The historical William Buckley was shipped out both as a convict and as a bricklayer, a mechanic, to build a new penal colony in what was decreed by the British Government to be "*terra nullius*": no one's land. One piece of William's workmanship survives, as fragments of a concrete armoury he built, which are now the crazy paving of a garden path in Ramsey Street. But William had brooded on other ideas.

He had long decided to walk back home. The possibility of this was a common belief among the convicts: head north along the coast, reach China, turn left, and there you were. They even drew compasses on scraps of paper, to keep them from going off course.

The land was so hostile, and fear of the Indians so great, that little attempt was made to recapture an escapee. Either he would come back, begging to be let into the camp, or he would never be seen again. Once William Buckley was out of range of the sentries he was presumed dead. After three months, the penal colony failed for lack of water, departed, and founded Hobart. The land was left to itself.

Meanwhile, William followed the coast to China.

Unfortunately, he was inside the narrow mouth of Port Phillip, the caldera of an extinct volcano. He did not know how to get food or water, and his progress was slow, his physical condition not good and worsening. After some ninety-five miles of walking in terrible conditions, he completed the circuit of Port Phillip and found himself looking across the entrance, straight at the ship and into the camp.

Among the photocopies that Ralph sent me was a critical edition of the ghosted first-person account of William's life in the bush, which was recorded by a hack journalist from Hobart after William's return to the whites. From this I was able to relate the Aboriginal names of physical features to their modern equivalents and could plot William's long journey.

Instead of giving up when he saw the penal colony he had staggered ninety-five miles to escape, he turned away and continued to head north-east for China. But he was travelling south-west.

This he continued to do for about two hundred miles. Then the text showed that he stopped, turned around, and set off, moving away from the sea, but in the right direction.

Why had he been 180 degrees out, and how had he come to discover his error? It is in the apparent anomalies that the most significant and exciting aspects of research are to be found. When I saw it, I felt time and space dissolve. I was with William Buckley, I was William Buckley, as I watched him work out his error. He had not realised that, in the Southern Hemisphere, in that mad land that seemed to have been designed to kill, where even the rivers were salt, the sun, at noon, was not in the south but in the north.

He made for China.

It had always been impossible. At last his body, after another two hundred miles and what must have been more than a year of solitary stumbling, dehydrated and starved, gave out. But his mind did not. He could not walk, so he crawled. He crawled until he came to a low hillock, and with fading vision, he saw a stick planted at the top of the hillock. A stick to help him to walk to China. He crawled for the stick, took hold of it, and, with that last effort he collapsed, and should have died.

He was found by a group of Aborigines. They had no knowledge of white men, but it was an Aboriginal belief that the dead became white. And here was this white giant, lying, not on a hillock but on the grave mound of a hero, warrior, wise man, healer and law-giver, Murrangurk; and he was holding not a stick but Murrangurk's spear. Murrangurk had come back to his People. It was as if Arthur had returned from Avalon.

For thirty-two years William Buckley was Murrangurk.

And here the anomalies began to pile up. It would be understandable that having made the journey from Tharangalkbek, the sky land, the gum-tree country, he would be in shock and have forgotten his language and his customs, but he would remember, given time. William had to have more going for him to be able to remain Murrangurk for thirty-two years. Also, I could infer something about Murrangurk.

Among Australian Aborigines, there is an unbreakable rule that when someone dies the name must never be spoken again. There is one exception. If the individual has been of the highest spiritual rank, that of shaman, the name may be spoken. So Murrangurk had been a shaman. Tough on William. Yet, thirty-two years later, the opportunistic British, who, within a few years exterminated the irritating niggers, often for sport, were saved by the authority of a Murrangurk who was very much respected, and wholly in control. What had started out as a twenty-year-old bricklayer was now a leader of thinkers and of warriors.

That for me, the novelist, was the crux, the conscious reason for writing the book. How was a priest-philosopher-healer-leader of great intelligence to communicate his wisdom in a language that no European spoke? How could his only point of contact, the Cheshire dialect and the convict Cant of an immature man, be used to tell what he knew?

It was historically impossible; and that is why the name of William Buckley has no place in Australia's list of folk heroes. Apart from his usefulness as an interpreter's being abused, and his laying of the first brick in what was to become Melbourne, he was discarded as a fellow of low intellect and brutish nature who had fallen instantly to the level of the heathen, to the extent that he had not even tried to introduce to them the Word of God. That perhaps William had had no need; that perhaps he had been initially the acolyte, would never have been countenanced.

And here I nearly foundered.

Ralph was in England and we were talking. I said that I had reached a point beyond which I could not go. For the first time, despite six years' work, I should have to abort a book. The impregnable barrier was the Aboriginal mind. I had no wish to invade their philosophy, which is largely sacred/secret, and is their last privacy and dignity, but unless I knew something of its truth my Aboriginal characters, and the change from William Buckley to Murrangurk, could not be shown as they naturally would have behaved as a result of reflecting, not revealing, the teachings of their esoteric culture. And there was no way in.

Ralph went home the next day. Shortly after, I had a letter from one of Australia's anthropologists: the leading one, for my purpose; because not only is she an anthropologist, but is a full member of an Aboriginal kinship group, is a female Elder, and of such high rank that she has the authority to adjudicate over both Men and Women's Matters. In her letter, she said that Ralph had told her that I was stuck, and she wanted to know whether she could help. She had a long-standing invitation to lecture in Lisbon, and the fee would pay her air-fare to Manchester.

And so I engaged with the Aboriginal mind among the throng and coloured neon of Manchester airport.

We recognised each other on sight, spontaneously broke into laughter, and, before we were clear of the car park ramps, she had begun. I continue to say "she", because of her wish to remain anonymous. Her work involves negotiating, finagling and manoeuvering for the pure Aborigines, and she prefers to keep a low profile. To me, she is lovingly known as The Southern Sybil.

Education in Aboriginal teaching is inferential, not, as with us, instructional. A pupil is shown something, or told a story, or given a statement in metaphorical images rather than through grammatical and syntactical logic; and, dependent on the reaction, is either moved forward or automatically returns to the start. It is akin to a fail-safe flow chart system of religious and philosophical wisdom. It is also a protection for the individual. We do not let people drive Formula I cars on the day they collect their driving licence.

As a result, Southern Sybil presents herself in such a way that the impatient, intolerant, inflexible (and therefore unsuitable) mind is irritated by what appears to be a deliberately elliptical, verbally dextrous and batty old woman. That is a serious, and often terminal, mistake. But stay with this Delphic nuisance, and things start to happen within oneself. A new grammar and syntax form. And thought takes a new shape, an Aboriginal shape. Once this is established, The Sybil uses both Hellenistic and Aboriginal models, both intellectually highly demanding, to express what has to be conveyed in the most efficient way.

I knew fairly soon that I had passed a crucial test, from an Aboriginal point of view, and I asked The Sybil why she had crossed the world on Ralph's say-so. "It was necessary," she said. "The only moment of doubt I had was when we were about to touch down at Manchester, and I thought: Dear God! What if he's not up to it? But when we both laughed before we spoke, I knew that we should dance well."

That was 1989. We have danced well. And the dance goes on, and will, for it has led me to see what has always given spring to my step, why the books are eternally different, eternally the same.

The Aborigine would call it my Dreaming, my song and my dance. The books are a vehicle for, and then marker of, the journey. It is why, once my duty towards them has been discharged, I have no further interest in them per se; which is not to claim that I disparage them. They are swept up, and still exist, in the cumulative intricacy and simplicity of the dance. Already *Strandloper* is taking its place, giving way to the new song that it has made possible by my writing of that portion of spiritual autobiography, with the help of so many people, foremost among whom are: Ralph Elliott, Southern Sybil, William Buckley, and particularly my wife and our children, who have had to live the soaking and the waiting.

The magpie must also be given his due. He is not quite the random thief that I may have made him. It is not by chance that he occurs as a principal in Aboriginal Creation myths. Without him, the book would not be as it is, nor would I be as spiritually enlarged as I feel myself to be.

I woke one morning with that imperative voice in my head. I had learnt that the voice is also known to the Aboriginal mind, and held as the source of inspiration. It is called The Voice that Thunders. It said: "Go to Marton church. Go now."

Marton church is not only the oldest timber framed church in Europe; it is the focal point of *Strandloper*. I went. And, as I entered the church I had known all my life, and consider to be one of the holy places of the world, I saw it through Aboriginal eyes for the first time, and was, as a human being, dumbfounded; and, as a writer, aware that all the cards had been finally dealt. An Aboriginal Elder, knowing nothing of architecture or of Christianity, would recognise Marton as sacred. For the magpie had discovered entoptic lines.

Entoptic lines were first published by two South African anthropologists, J. D. Lewis-Wilson and T. A. Dowson, in *Current Anthropology*, in 1988. They had noticed that the same abstract patterns tended to appear in all preliterate art and iconography, in all places and at all times, from the Upper Palaeolithic cave paintings of France and Spain to the modern religious art of the Kalahari bushmen. There are about six patterns, and they are invariable: zigzag, cross-hatching, honeycomb, carinate, dot, and circle/spiral. Lewis-Wilson and Dowson consulted neurologists who reported the same patterns, which are found in three conditions of the human brain. They appear to be projected as external images by people entering *grand mal* epileptic seizures; by many migraineurs; and as the result of shamans entering trance or ecstatic states. The ritual body painting of Aboriginal adepts and the abstractions of the stained-glass windows of mediaeval Marton are the same. Both William Buckley and Murrangurk would have known them. What I had been expecting, a Green Man, or foliate head, disguised, our daughter found later. No composer of *Strandloper* could have wished for more. The entoptic lines created the jacket of the book; and they made the climax of the story.

At the start, I dodged the question of why I have written by saying that I had no choice. But why no choice? Only with *Strandloper* have the last forty years become wholly clear.

I am a member of a family of rural craftsmen, but I use my hands in a different way. I have spent those forty years in trying to celebrate the land and tongue of a culture that has been marginalised by a metropolitan intellectualism, that churns out canonical prose through writers who seem unable to allow new concepts or to integrate the diversity of our language; who draw on the library, ignorant of the land; on the head, bereft of the heart; making of fair speech mere rustic conversation; so that I am led to ask: have we become so lazy that we have lost the will to read our own language, except at its most anodyne, and, from that reading, too lazy to create? For true reading is creativity: the willingness to look into the open hand of the writer and to see what may, or may not, be there. A writer's job is to offer.

There were two spurs to my endeavour. The first was the realisation that a well-meaning teacher had washed my mouth out with carbolic soap when I was five years old for what she called "talking broad", which she did not know was the language of one of the treasures of English poetry. The second was that the earliest surviving example, which may have been the sum of his literacy, of writing by a Garner: the signature of another William: is a slashed, fierce cross made with the anger of a pen held in the fist as a dagger.

"There is only the fight to recover what has been lost," T. S. Eliot says in "East Coker". "The rest is not our business."

So it was gratifying when a Professor of Humanities at St Louis University wrote: "There is, in [*Strandloper*], a kind of thesis . . . about how a precious mythology was allowed to slip by a controlling politico-literary agenda. . . . But most of all, there is a refusal to grieve. . . . The people are dead, but the words lie like stones, indestructible as the land, and as invincible."

To have been able to use my indoctrination into academe as a means to free a suppressed, concrete voice, to give a slashed cross a flowing hand, opened to offer our starved and arid prose if but one way out of the library, back to its enriching soil, has been a privilege and an apprenticeship.

That apprenticeship: the quest from gash and slash of a cross, by way of carbolic soap, to the Voice that Thunders, is over. Now, I can begin. Indeed, I already have.

Appendix

Oral History & Applied Archaeology in Cheshire

There are two methods of making astronomical calculations from maps that are accurate enough for the purposes of archaeology. The second is the more complex, but is needed when the use of more than one map is called for.

An important measurement is the azimuth of the sun at rising and at setting. The azimuth, A, is associated with the declination, δ, by the equation:

$$\cos A = \frac{\sin \delta - \sin \phi \sin h}{\cos \phi \cos h}$$

ϕ is the latitude of the observer and h is the altitude of the sun.

Some correction is always needed, since the viewed rising and setting points of astronomical objects are not exactly where the equation shows, because of a number of physical distortions.

One is the refraction of light. The sun's, or moon's, light is bent by the atmosphere, so that the sun appears to be higher than it is above the horizon. This bending varies under differing conditions, but is about $0.55°$ at the horizon. Refraction makes the time of rising appear earlier, so decreasing the azimuth, and the setting later, increasing the azimuth.

A correction for parallax, unnecessary for the sun, must always be made for the moon, which is about $0.95°$. Parallax works in the apparently opposite way to refraction.

The height of the horizon must also be included. When a long distance is involved, the angular elevation (plus or minus) of the horizon should be reduced to allow for the curvature of the Earth, at a rate of 0.0027961° per statute mile of the distance from the observer to the horizon.

Therefore, the full value of h, when used, is:
h = (horizon altitude) − (curvature of the Earth correction)
+ (parallax correction) − (refraction).

This will give the azimuth when the centre of the disc is on the horizon. For the azimuth of first flash, at the rising, or last instant, at the setting, the value of h must be corrected by 0.25°.

To find the azimuths of sunrise and sunset at an archaeological site; then let $\delta = \epsilon$, using the value of ϵ for the date of the site, and correct h as described. For summer rising, let $\delta = + \epsilon$. If the azimuth that is found is subtracted from 360°, it will give the summer setting. For winter rising, let $\delta = - \epsilon$. The azimuth will lie between 90° and 180°, but, if subtracted from 360°, the setting azimuth will be given.

Alternatively, when the map coordinates of two points are known, the azimuth of the line joining them can be calculated, and the distance between them. The distance is needed for the working out of the angles of altitude.

Following A. Thom, let λ_c L_c, be the latitude and longitude of the observer at C and λ_d L_d be the same coordinates for the observed point D.

$\Delta\lambda = \lambda_d - \lambda_c$,

$\Delta L = L_d - L_c$, (east longitude reckoned positive),

$\lambda_m = \frac{1}{2}(\lambda_d + \lambda_c) = $ mean altitude.

A = required azimuth measured clockwise from north.

Find $\tan \phi$ from: $\tan \phi = K \cos \lambda_m \Delta L / \Delta\lambda$, which gives ϕ.

Find ΔA from: $\Delta A = \Delta L \sin \lambda_m$ and the azimuth of D from C is $A = \phi - \frac{1}{2}\Delta A$.

If the Earth were a sphere, K would be unity. To allow for its being an oblate spheroid, K may be taken to vary from 1.0028 in latitude 50° to 1.0017 in latitude 60°.

The distance CD in statute miles is:

$$c = CD = 0.01922\Delta\lambda/\cos\phi \text{ or } 0.01926\Delta L\cos\lambda_m/\sin\phi.$$

To calculate the apparent angle of altitude of D as seen from C in terms of the distance, c, between them and the amount by which D is higher than C, the curvature of the Earth must be allowed for, as must the refraction that bends the light between D and C. Then:

$$h = H/c - c(1 - 2k)/2R,$$

where H = height of D above C,

c = distance of D from C,

R = radius of curvature of the spheroid,

k = coefficient of refraction.

k is usually 0.075 for rays passing over land, and 0.081 for rays passing over the sea.

Let H be given in feet, c in statute miles, and h in minutes of arc. Then:

$$h = 0.65H/c - 0.37c$$

Since delivering this paper, my confidence in my ability to handle lunar calculations has more than waned. However, I have left them as first observed, so that a more competent mathematician may repudiate, or confirm, the statements. If I have erred, it does not change the main thrust of the argument, or cause to dematerialise the stone axe.

ALAN GARNER, *January* 1997